Praise for The Unofficial Disney Parks Cookbook Series

"Better than a FastPass."
—*BuzzFeed*

"Sure to satisfy anyone's Disney Park cravings….
Will make your family and friends' dreams come true."
—*Reader's Digest*

"One of the best gifts for Disney fans."
—*The Hollywood Reporter*

"Just as good as being there."
—*Today.com*

"Will transport you directly into Disneyland."
—*Business Insider*

"The perfect gift to give your Disney-loving foodie friends for the holidays."
—*Elite Daily*

"It's the most magical cookbook I own."
—*Insider*

"If your mind was boggled and your taste buds blown by the sheer creativity, gorgeous photos, and just plain entertaining history and food facts of *The Unofficial Disney Parks Cookbook*, then you will be no less blown away by Ashley Craft's follow-up, *The Unofficial Disney Parks Drink Recipe Book*. From refreshing (Strawberry Acqua Fresca) to unusual (Blurrgfire) to comforting (Black Spire Hot Chocolate) to decadent (Brooklyn Blackout), these drinks evoke the magic and fun of the Disney Parks for young and old and everyone in between. Excuse me while I go into my kitchen to whip up some Frozen Sunshine."
—Dinah Bucholz, author of the *New York Times* bestseller *The Unofficial Harry Potter Cookbook*

"What EVERY Disney fan needs in their life…seriously magic!"
—*Domestic Geek Girl*

"A drink here for everyone in the family."
—*The Disney Food Blog*

"If you loved the bestselling *The Unofficial Disney Parks Cookbook*, you need the newest version with recipes from EPCOT."
—*SheKnows*

"Gorgeous book…unique and easy recipes."
—*Variety*

"It's the perfect way to satisfy that Disney craving…whenever it beckons."
—*Yahoo! Life*

"Better than a trip to the Park."
—*PureWow*

Adams Media
An Imprint of Simon & Schuster, Inc.
100 Technology Center Drive
Stoughton, Massachusetts 02072

Copyright © 2023 by Ashley Craft.

All rights reserved, including the right to reproduce this book or portions thereof in any form whatsoever. For information, address Adams Media Subsidiary Rights Department, 1230 Avenue of the Americas, New York, NY 10020.

First Adams Media hardcover edition September 2023

ADAMS MEDIA and colophon are trademarks of Simon & Schuster.

For information about special discounts for bulk purchases, please contact Simon & Schuster Special Sales at 1-866-506-1949 or business@simonandschuster.com.

The Simon & Schuster Speakers Bureau can bring authors to your live event. For more information or to book an event, contact the Simon & Schuster Speakers Bureau at 1-866-248-3049 or visit our website at www.simonspeakers.com.

Interior design by Sylvia McArdle
Photographs by Harper Point Photography
Photography chefs: Kira Friedman, Martine English, Christine Tarango
Interior illustrations by Russell Tate; © Simon & Schuster, Inc.
Maps by Russell Tate
Images © 123RF

Manufactured in China

10 9 8 7 6 5 4 3 2 1

Library of Congress Cataloging-in-Publication Data
Names: Craft, Ashley, author.
Title: The unofficial Disney Parks restaurants cookbook / Ashley Craft, Author of the USA TODAY Bestselling the unofficial Disney Parks cookbook.
Description: Stoughton, Massachusetts: Adams Media, 2023. | Series: Unofficial cookbook | Includes index.
Identifiers: LCCN 2022056121 | ISBN 9781507220351 (hc) | ISBN 9781507220368 (ebook)
Subjects: LCSH: Disney, Walt, 1901–1966. | Cooking--California--Disneyland. | Disneyland (Calif.) | LCGFT: Cookbooks.
Classification: LCC TX715.2.C34 C73 2023 | DDC 641.59794--dc23/eng/20221122
LC record available at https://lccn.loc.gov/2022056121

ISBN 978-1-5072-2035-1
ISBN 978-1-5072-2036-8 (ebook)

Many of the designations used in this book, including but not limited to place names and character names, are registered trademarks of The Walt Disney Company. Where those designations appear in this book and the publisher was aware of the trademark status, the designations have been printed with initial capital letters.

Always follow safety and commonsense cooking protocols while using kitchen utensils, operating ovens and stoves, and handling uncooked food. If children are assisting in the preparation of any recipe, they should always be supervised by an adult.

The
UNOFFICIAL
Disney Parks Restaurants
COOKBOOK

From CAFE ORLEANS's Battered & Fried Monte Cristo
to HOLLYWOOD & VINE's Caramel Monkey Bread,
100 MAGICAL DISHES from the Best
•••••• Disney Dining Destinations ••••••

ASHLEY CRAFT
Author of the *USA TODAY* Bestselling *The Unofficial Disney Parks Cookbook*

ADAMS MEDIA
NEW YORK   LONDON   TORONTO   SYDNEY   NEW DELHI

Contents

Preface 9
Introduction 10

PART 1
Disney Parks Restaurants 101 ... 13

CHAPTER 1
The Disney Parks Restaurants Experience ... 15

The Compelling Force of Disney Foods 16
A Closer Look at Disney Restaurants 17
Creating Disney Restaurant Experiences at Home 23

CHAPTER 2
The Disney Parks Cook's Essentials ... 25

PART 2
Disney Parks Restaurant Recipes ... 37

CHAPTER 3
Breakfast ... 39

American Breakfast Burrito 41	Mickey-Shaped Pancakes 49
Mustafarian Lava Rolls 42	Cinnamon-Sugar Doughnuts 50
Breakfast Sandwich 44	Classique Galettes 51
Sausage and Gravy Tots 45	Melba Crêpes 53
Cinnamon Rolls 46	Breakfast Bowls 54

Warm Glazed Doughnut 55
Marshall's Favorite Sausage, Egg, and Cheese Biscuits 56
Avocado Toast...................... 58
Ever-Expanding Cinna-Pym Toast ...61
Slow-Roasted Ham, Swiss & Egg Croissants 62
Caramel Monkey Bread............. 64

CHAPTER 4

Lunch . . . 65

Chieftain Chicken Skewers.......... 66
Outback Vegetable Skewers........ 67
Ronto-Less Garden Wraps.......... 69
Declaration Salad....................71
The Sun Bonnet Trio Strawberry Salad............................... 72
Our Famous Cobb Salad............ 73
Peanut Butter, Chocolate-Hazelnut Spread, and Banana Sandwich...... 75
Lobster Bisque 76

Orange Chicken..................... 78
Margherita Flatbreads 81
"Totchos" 82
Shrimp Salad Roll 84
Lettuce Cups........................ 86
Poblano Mac & Cheese.............. 87
Smokehouse Chicken Salad 88
Not So Little Chicken Sandwich......91

CHAPTER 5

Appetizers and Snacks . . . 93

Fried Pickles....................... 94
Five-Blossom Bread................. 97
Pomme Frites 99
Country Seasonal Salad 100
House-Made Peach Applesauce.... 102
Carpaccio di Manzo................ 103
Chicken Pot Stickers 105
Fried Mozzarella................... 106
Baby Iceberg Wedge Salad 107

Spoon Bread...................... 108
Parmesan Chips 109
Fried Herb and Garlic Cheese...... 110
Candied Bacon.....................113
Ahi Tuna Nachos 114
Frijoles Charros 116
Tiffins Signature Bread Service.....117
Lobster Nachos.................... 120

CHAPTER 6

Main Dishes ... 123

Plaza Inn Specialty Chicken 125	Pork on Pork Burger 138
Jambalaya 127	Slow-Roasted Sliced Grilled Beef Bowls................................ 140
Battered & Fried Monte Cristo 128	
Herb-Salted Pork Tenderloin....... 130	Felucian Kefta and Hummus Garden Spread 141
Tenderloin of Beef...................131	
Curry-Spiced Pizza................. 133	St. Louis Rib Dinners............... 144
Cranberry Roasted Medallion of Angus Beef Filet................. 135	Hot Link Bowls 146
	Beef Bulgogi Burritos 147
Vegetable Korma 136	Impossible Spoonful............... 149
Savoyarde Galette 137	Ka-Cheeseburger................... 150

CHAPTER 7

Desserts ... 153

Mine Cart Brownies 154	Grapefruit Cake..................... 169
Sweet Lumpia!..................... 155	Wookiee Cookies 172
House-Made Chocolate-Chunk Cookie Sundaes 156	Fried Wontons 175
	Chocolate Cake 176
Ooey Gooey Toffee Cake 159	Honey Bee Cupcakes............... 179
Butterscotch Pudding 160	Strawberry Shortcake Funnel Cake Fries 181
The Sword in the Sweet.............161	
Johnny Appleseed's Warm Apple Cakes 164	Celestial-Sized Candy Bar: Choco-Smash CANDY Bar 184
Vegan Blackberry Cupcakes........ 166	Hazelnut Crunch Mickey Pops...... 187
Berry Short Cake................... 168	

CHAPTER 8
Drinks...189

Cold Brew Black Caf 190
Yub Nub 192
Meiloorun Juice 193
Hurricane Cocktail................ 194
Happy Haunts Milk Shake 197
Adventureland Colada 198
Lightyear Lemonade................ 199
Black Magic.......................200
Violet Silk Martini...................202

Orbiting Oreos.....................204
Mowie Wowie.......................205
Fichwa Maji.......................207
Rum Blossoms......................208
Pingo Doce 209
Proton Punch......................210
Honey Buzz........................ 213
2319.............................. 214

Disney Parks Recipe Locations..215
Standard US/Metric Measurement Conversions................................228
Index...230

Acknowledgments

Thank you, Danny, for your continued support and encouragement in my writing career. Love you! You're the best partner, unofficial editor, and friend anyone could ask for.

Special thanks to my research assistants for this book: my sister and niece, Jamie and Ellie Giles, and my parents, Karen and Jeff Peterson, for coming to Walt Disney World and Disneyland to tackle the difficult task of dining at so many restaurants. We made amazing memories and experienced really tasty food.

And a very special thank-you to my Disney College Program buddies, Haley Hemphill and Ariel Letts. You spent so much time offering great ideas for this book. Thank you, thank you! I hope you'll continue to help me in many books to come.

Thanks to the best team in publishing: Joe Perry, Julia Jacques, Sarah Doughty, and Mary Kate Schulte for all your help in creating and promoting my books!

Preface

When I was a kid growing up in Anaheim Hills, California, visiting Disneyland was a common occurrence, but the magic never dulled. Even after visiting week after week, I always looked forward to passing through those gates and crossing under the train tracks to enter Main Street, U.S.A. The sights treated my young self to exciting fantasies of princesses, pirates, and favorite characters from newly released movies (like *Beauty and the Beast* or *The Lion King*). Our visits were full of riding the hottest attractions and catching the latest nighttime spectacular.

As an adult, and subsequently as a theme park cookbook author, I am still going on the rides and watching the parades, but my Disney Parks trips primarily revolve around a different element of Disney magic: the food. When I was writing *The Unofficial Disney Parks Cookbook*, snacks and treats were the focus. And while snacks and treats are amazing and are great bites when you're on the go, nothing beats having a reservation at a Disney restaurant. You can get out of the sun and have an unhurried meal of incredible chef-made concoctions. Each of the restaurants is impeccably themed and not only delivers succulent dishes and drinks but also tells a story not found anywhere else in the Parks. Now eating at a restaurant at Disney is the highlight of each Park day, and I plan everything around that! I get giddy just thinking about stepping into Jungle Navigation Co. LTD Skipper Canteen and taking a gander at its butterfly wall in the library while sipping on an Adventureland Colada, or listening to the wafting panpipe music at Yak & Yeti Restaurant as I finish off the last bits of my Fried Wontons after a magnificent meal.

As exciting as dining at Disney is, it can also be challenging. It can be hard to get reservations, your day might already be scheduled, you may not be ready to drop a lot of money on top of an already pricey trip, or you may have children who just won't sit still. Not to mention the days when you would love to enjoy a meal from your favorite location, but don't have plans to visit the Parks anytime soon. Now you can enjoy the incredible cuisine of the Disney Parks in your own home without breaking the bank.

Introduction

Disney Parks are well known for their incredible rides and world-class entertainment. But it isn't just about what you see or do during your Disney day that makes it so magical—it's also what you eat! Disney restaurants offer dishes and sips that are not only tasty on their own but also fit within the themes of their specific areas of the Parks. You can feel like the aristocracy of 1700s France at Be Our Guest Restaurant—and like you have flown out of Earth's atmosphere at Space 220 Restaurant!

The Unofficial Disney Parks Restaurants Cookbook contains one hundred of the most iconic restaurant offerings from all six US Disney Parks. With dozens of restaurants across Disneyland, Disney California Adventure, Magic Kingdom, EPCOT, Disney's Hollywood Studios, and Disney's Animal Kingdom, the flavors are endless and the menus are often changing to include even more options and swap out different recipes according to season or simply a chef's whim. And now you can enjoy some of the most popular dishes and drinks from these beloved locations right at home! Organized by course, the chapters feature recipes currently or previously offered at both Quick Service and Table Service Disney restaurants, including:

- Breakfasts to prepare you for the day ahead, like the Mustafarian Lava Rolls from Oga's Cantina and Avocado Toast from Pacific Wharf Café.
- Lunches that satisfy, including the famous Lobster Bisque soup from Coral Reef Restaurant and Chieftain Chicken Skewers from Bengal Barbecue.
- Appetizers and snacks for every mood, like the Fried Pickles from Carnation Café and Parmesan Chips from Fairfax Fare.

- Savory main dishes, such as the luxurious Cranberry Roasted Medallion of Angus Beef Filet from Club 33 and the more laid-back Curry-Spiced Pizza from Connections Eatery.
- Desserts to finish a meal in style, like The Sword in the Sweet from Cinderella's Royal Table and Grapefruit Cake from The Hollywood Brown Derby.
- Beverages for all occasions, like the family-friendly Lightyear Lemonade from Space 220 Restaurant and the adult-approved Rum Blossoms from Pongu Pongu.

There are simple and easy dishes to whip up in a snap, as well as more-involved treats to impress family and friends.

But before you tie on that Cinderella apron or pull out those mixing bowls, be sure to read through Part 1 to learn more about the Disney restaurants featured in Part 2, as well as what kitchen tools and pantry staples you'll want to have on hand.

What are you waiting for? Turn the page and let's whip up a big helping of Disney magic!

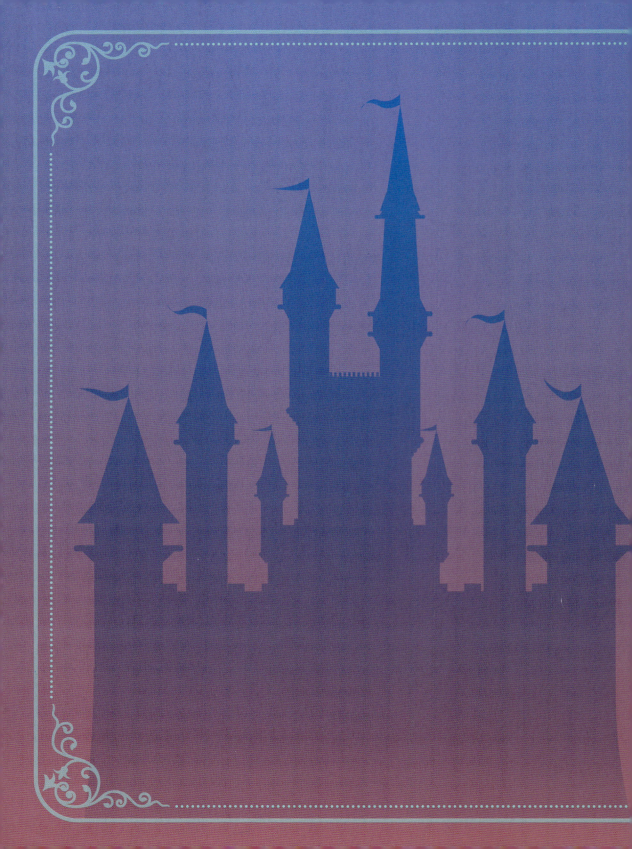

······· PART 1 ·······

Disney Parks Restaurants 101

Disney Parks are known for their churros and Dole Whips, but they are also quickly gaining in popularity with their restaurants. Nothing beats a reservation at a nice, air-conditioned establishment to break up a long Park day! And with dozens of restaurants across the US Disney Parks, the choices for cuisine and atmosphere are plentiful.

In this part, you'll find everything you need to make the recipes in Part 2. In Chapter 1, you'll explore some of the most popular restaurants in the six US Parks: Disneyland, Disney California Adventure, Magic Kingdom, EPCOT, Disney's Hollywood Studios, and Disney's Animal Kingdom. Discover how these beloved locations have become irresistible to Park-goers, and what kinds of dishes and beverages you can find in each one. Then, in Chapter 2, take a peek at the equipment you will want to have on hand to create the recipes in Part 2. The tools detailed here will help you make dishes and drinks that are worthy of a certain mouse. The tasty magic of Disney restaurants awaits; let's dig in!

····· **CHAPTER 1** ·······

The Disney Parks Restaurants Experience

Most Disney Parks guests have come to know and love the food. And eating at Disney provides way more than just sustenance. The restaurants are a fully immersive experience, from the sights and sounds to the tastes and smells. Each restaurant has a story to tell!

In this chapter, you'll learn more about the unique experiences created at popular Disney restaurants, from ambiance to the kinds of themes at play in the different meals and drinks. With this knowledge in hand, you can either visit a Disney restaurant and enjoy the experience there or re-create the experience in your home with the recipes in Part 2! Either way, you'll be ready to embrace your Disney side and make dining a fun and delicious adventure covered in pixie dust.

THE COMPELLING FORCE OF DISNEY FOODS

Disney has been serving iconic culinary offerings from day one (July 15, 1955). Popcorn, churros, frozen beverages, hot dogs, and fried chicken are just a few of the foods that Walt chose for the opening of Disneyland that still exist in the Parks today. And while those offerings remain some of the biggest sellers, Disney Parks have greatly expanded their snack, meal, dessert, and drink choices to include an array of cuisines as big as you can imagine.

Disney Parks break down the types of dining into five distinct categories. The very top and finest cuisine at Disney is served at Signature Table Service restaurants. This category includes character dining experiences (when friends like Mickey, Minnie, or Princesses visit you at your table) and fancier restaurants. Next down the ladder are Table Service restaurants, which have hosts, servers, and reserved seating, but aren't as expensive as Signature dining and don't have character experiences. Then you have Quick Service restaurants. These are a lot like fast-food restaurants found outside the Parks, where you order at a counter (or make a mobile order), pick up your food, and find a table where you can sit and eat. Quick Service restaurants have designated seating areas and provide enough seating for everyone who wants to dine there, but you can also choose to eat your food on the go or at other seating locations. Next are permanent Snack Stands, where a small window and counter provide a limited selection of snacks, treats, and beverages, and very little seating exists (if at all). Lastly are mobile or semi-mobile Snack Carts that serve popcorn, pre-packaged ice cream treats, and sodas. These are scattered all over the Parks and usually have no designated seating available.

The Unofficial Disney Parks Cookbook mostly provided recipes from Snack Carts, Snack Stands, and the occasional Quick Service restaurant. This book, however, focuses on Signature Table Service, Table Service, and Quick Service restaurants across the US Disney Parks. Broken down by meal type, this layout makes it easier for you to find something for whatever you're in the mood for. If you do want to find a particular item by what Park it is from, simply take a look at the maps included in the back of this book.

A CLOSER LOOK AT DISNEY RESTAURANTS

Because of the variety of dining locations across the Parks, you can be eating Thanksgiving dinner any day of the year at Liberty Tree Tavern, and then watch underwater life at Coral Reef Restaurant. Or maybe you're parked in a car sipping a milkshake at Sci-Fi Dine-In Theater Restaurant or feasting on space meats from Docking Bay 7 Food and Cargo.

While every one of the Disney restaurants is special and has its own story to tell, let's take a deeper look into a few specific Disney restaurants and what makes them so irresistible and unique. This sampling serves to intrigue your palate and show more of the elements behind the different Signature Table Service, Table Service, and Quick Service options in the Disney Parks.

Be Our Guest Restaurant

Be Our Guest Restaurant is all about *Beauty and the Beast*, from the decor on the walls all the way down to the servers wearing outfits reminiscent of those worn by the turned-human servants in the movie. The chance to not only step inside a beloved movie but also taste the flavors the characters taste is a special opportunity. And in what better way than with the food so famously presented by Lumière in one of the most memorable animated musical scenes of all time, "Be Our Guest"?

Be Our Guest Restaurant opened at Magic Kingdom in 2012 with the "New Fantasyland" expansion that included Under the Sea ~ Journey of the Little Mermaid and the Storybook Circus area. Designed to take guests inside Beast's Castle, three themed rooms are available to dine in: The Grand Ballroom, The Castle Gallery, and The West Wing. While each room serves the same cuisine, the theming sets the mood for your meal.

The restaurant originally began as a Quick Service restaurant, but had a few key differences. As with all Quick Service restaurants, guests would order their meals at a counter, but a Cast Member would hand you a rose puck to take with you to your table. Once you chose your seat in one of the three dining rooms, a Cast Member would magically find you across the restaurant, or with some GPS wizardry hidden within the rose puck, who's to say?

Due to its immense popularity, people were lined up out the castle doors and around the walkways just to dine at the restaurant. So, in an unprecedented shift, Be Our Guest Restaurant changed from a Quick Service restaurant to a Signature Table Service restaurant with a three-course "dining experience" and a fixed price tag per adult or child. Now guests need to make an advance reservation to ensure a seat at a table and have a high-end menu to choose from—including Escargot de Bourgogne, Herb-salted Pork Tenderloin, and a rich Dessert Trio to top off the meal. What used to be a somewhat quick bite is now a whole experience complete with an occasional visit by the Beast himself.

Space 220 Restaurant

Shifting gears not just to another Park, but to another stratosphere, let's talk about one of the hottest restaurants at Disney Parks—Space 220. Opened in fall 2021, it has been one of the most coveted reservations to get since it launched. And *launched* is truly the right word because this restaurant takes you on a trip like no other.

When you enter the restaurant, a Cast Member will give you a colored boarding pass and you'll wait until your boarding color is called. Then you'll file into a small circular "Stellarvator" fitted with "windows" on the floor and ceiling. After a countdown, you'll feel and see the "Stellarvator" take off on a pole (seemingly) 220 miles long that delivers you to a space station anchored above Earth. Once you disembark the "Stellarvator," a rotating vegetable garden greets you before the main event: the windowed dining room. Wrapped in floor-to-ceiling windows that look out into "space," you'll see a huge view of Earth—and might even catch a glimpse of some other space travelers passing by.

Now of course, The Walt Disney Company did not invent a new instant space travel that you can experience only at a theme park. It is an elaborate illusion, and they absolutely pull it off. You truly do feel like you're moving upward in the "Stellarvator" (even though it doesn't actually leave the ground at all), and the view out of the dining room windows is so stunning, you may need to hold on to something as the sensation of floating through space is so strong. It is no wonder that everyone is clamoring to get inside this restaurant.

Disney could have stopped right there and just had the joy of this restaurant tied to the view, but they created a fully incredible experience by serving top-notch foods as well. Diners are given a menu to choose from a two-course list (Lift-Offs and Star Course) with optional desserts and drinks available. The flavors are out of this world and will delight a variety of palates. There are also several vegan and gluten-free dishes, such as the Galaxy Grain Salad and the Coconut Panna Cotta. While the "Stellarvator" and view out the windows will bring you into this restaurant the first time, the succulent foods will bring you back again and again. This Signature Table Service experience stands apart from the rest by merging the ideas of "attraction" and "dining" into one unforgettable experience.

Tiffins Restaurant

The next restaurant discussed in this chapter stands apart for a whole other reason. Tiffins Restaurant at Disney's Animal Kingdom is a unique Signature Table Service location that brings together the creators and the created into a special space.

Named after the metal lunch boxes carried by travelers, Tiffins Restaurant pays homage to the Imagineers that created Disney's Animal Kingdom. Each of the walls and ceilings is dotted with authentic memorabilia gathered by Imagineers on their adventures overseas while studying the various countries and cultures to represent at Disney's Animal Kingdom. Each of the three dining rooms offers a theme: Africa, Asia, and Exotic Animals. Be sure to take a walk around the restaurant and check out each room so you don't miss anything!

Most of the Disney Parks aim to pull you into an illusion and make you feel as if you really are in the particular place or time they are trying to construct. Tiffins Restaurant does the opposite, pulling back the curtain and allowing guests a peek at the process of making all of those other spaces come to life. The people who strive so hard to make Disney Parks the special experience they are get a limelight of their own.

And if you can't get a reservation to Tiffins Restaurant, no worries! Simply walk up to the doors and ask if there are any seats available at Nomad Lounge. This lounge is adjacent to the restaurant and also holds special

Imagineering goodies to check out. Both the restaurant and the lounge have menus with authentic African and Asian cuisine; there is something for everyone. The Tiffins Signature Bread Service pairs breads of the world with flavorful dips, is perfect for sharing, and is available in the restaurant and the lounge. Other popular dishes include the Whole-fried Sustainable Fish and Tamarind-braised Short Rib. Guests love the sweet taste of vegan Churros with Vanilla Crema and Coffee Crème Anglaise at Nomad Lounge. You can find Tiffins Restaurant along the trail from Discovery Island to Pandora—The World of Avatar.

50's Prime Time Café

Moving along to Disney's Hollywood Studios, we have a Table Service restaurant that all Park-goers can enjoy. Next to Echo Lake near the front of the Park, 50's Prime Time Café is a bit reminiscent of a 1950s-style house. Some tables even have old tube TVs showing black-and-white shows. The food is delicious old-fashioned American fare, including fried chicken, collard greens, and milkshakes.

But it isn't the decor or even the food that really drives the popularity: It is the Cast Members working here. Unlike most dining establishments that pride themselves on polite and attentive waitstaff, 50's Prime Time Café hosts a whole team of servers whose job is to be as "friendly" with their guests as aunts and uncles are to their nieces and nephews. In fact, they are often downright rude when it comes to making eaters finish their vegetables or wash their hands after using the restroom. And this is what guests come here for! The blunt-talking service leaves adults and kids howling with laughter as Cast Members refuse to serve dessert until all the collard greens are finished or proclaim to the whole restaurant that you'll have to put plastic sheets on the bed after how many soda refills you've had.

This clever move has made the restaurant stand out as a favorite of guests at Disney's Hollywood Studios. In fact, servers at Whispering Canyon Cafe at Disney's Wilderness Lodge have followed suit and deliver a similar style of comedy in a western family-style setting.

Docking Bay 7 Food and Cargo

Guests may tend to look toward the Signature and Table Service restaurants for the most immersive theming and highest-quality food, but at Disney, even the Quick Service restaurants deliver an unforgettable ambiance and tasty food—at a more affordable price. This is especially true in the newest lands of Walt Disney World, Star Wars: Galaxy's Edge and Pandora—The World of Avatar. At their flagship dining locations, you order at the counter or on your phone, similar to at your favorite fast-food restaurant. But unlike quick-service chains outside the Parks, these restaurants send out their food on reusable dinnerware themed perfectly to their surroundings.

A favorite stop in Star Wars: Galaxy's Edge, Docking Bay 7 Food and Cargo is nestled in the heart of Black Spire Outpost on the planet of Batuu. Serving smuggler, scum, and space pilot alike, this restaurant has something for everyone—like the Felucian Kefta Garden and Hummus Spread for hard-working Twi'leks, and Ithorian Pasta Rings for the littlest younglings. Decor is marked by a working-class vibe with a homey feel lent by the alcoves you can eat in as you privately discuss galactic shipments. You won't even be missing a Table Service meal in Galaxy's Edge by the time you lick your spork clean.

Satu'li Canteen

Another Quick Service location you shouldn't miss is Satu'li Canteen in Pandora—The World of Avatar. This is the best place to grab a bite to eat if you're stationed in the Valley of Mo'ara in Pandora. As the name suggests, the canteen has a cafeteria-like atmosphere (if a cafeteria were in the middle of a luscious valley in a faraway planet, of course). Some of the foods have flavors from back on Earth, like the Cheeseburger Steamed Pods, but with an otherworldly look only Pandora can pull off. Simple staples, like chicken and beef, are paired with inventive and flavorful sauces that elevate the dishes to theme park favorites. It's no wonder the seating overflows out onto the patio to accommodate all the hungry guests of the Valley!

Club 33

There is one restaurant in the Disney Parks that stands apart from the categories of Signature Table Service, Table Service, and Quick Service: the fabulously unique Club 33. When Walt Disney created Disneyland in Anaheim, California, he wanted a clean and wholesome place for families to have fun together. But that didn't eliminate the fact that he also needed a space to schmooze investors and thrill dignitaries and celebrities when they were at Disneyland. Modeled after the corporate and VIP lounges of the World's Fair, Club 33 opened shortly after Walt's death in 1967 and gave The Walt Disney Company a place to invite people such as Disney sponsors. Disneyland also offered individual memberships to the club.

Club 33 can be accessed only by members and their guests, and the waiting list to join can be yearslong. The initial membership fee is around $25–$35,000, with annual dues in the $10–$20,000 range. On top of that, diners *still* pay $100–$200 per person per meal at Club 33. So, for a majority of Park-goers, this is a reservation that sits unchecked in many a bucket list. (Don't worry, though! Part 2 includes a taste of this exclusive restaurant that you can enjoy at home.)

Club 33 used to be a singular experience at Disneyland but has since expanded. Now there are similar club locations; for example, 1901 is in the Carthay Circle building at Disney California Adventure. Others are at Magic Kingdom (Adventureland), EPCOT (The American Adventure pavilion), Disney's Hollywood Studios (above The Hollywood Brown Derby), and Disney's Animal Kingdom (Harambe). Each one has similar admission requirements and is tucked away from the public eye.

Of course, the food at Club 33 and its sister clubs is exquisite, fresh, and expertly crafted by a team of illustrious chefs. The menus change to include seasonal items, such as the Cranberry Roasted Medallion of Angus Beef Filet, and the waitstaff is ready to accommodate all requests made by diners. If you get the chance to visit, keep an eye open for celebrities or other familiar faces! It's where all the coolest VIPs have their lunch or dinner while at Disneyland.

CREATING DISNEY RESTAURANT EXPERIENCES AT HOME

Disney restaurants are special places that deliver special experiences. And the core of these experiences is the food. It is the incredible flavors and huge array of dishes and sips that keep guests coming back and asking for more.

This cookbook gives you the opportunity to make your home a more magical place where the flavors of Disney are wafting through the air and family and friends can gather and make new, delicious memories—no Park ticket or VIP membership needed. Where will dinner be tonight? In the halls of Beast's Castle? In space? Will dessert pay homage to your favorite princess? Or a certain lovable Wookiee? Why not make a stop in Tokyo with a luscious cocktail (or mocktail)? In your kitchen, you're the architect of your own culinary story!

CHAPTER 2

The Disney Parks Cook's Essentials

Now that you know *why* Disney Parks restaurant food and drinks are so alluring, it's time to get ready to make them yourself! In this chapter, the equipment you'll need to cook the recipes in this book is explored in detail. But don't get overwhelmed! Most of these items are probably already in your own kitchen, or there may be an easy substitution you can use if you don't have something. So be sure to read through this chapter before you move on to the recipes in Part 2.

Once you've taken a look, you'll be prepared to become the head chef of your own kitchen, crafting Disney magic right before your very eyes!

AIR FRYER

An air fryer reaches high temperatures and circulates heat quickly within a compact space in order to crisp up foods, giving them a "fried" taste. Don't have an air fryer? Just use your standard oven and cook as instructed. You may need to add more time, so keep an eye on the food as it cooks.

ALUMINUM CREAM MAKER

An aluminum cream maker expedites the whipped cream–making process and allows flavored creams to be made in seconds. If you don't have one, you can order one from an online retailer, or you can simply whip the cream using the whisk attachment of a stand mixer, or whip it by hand with a whisk.

BACON PRESS

Used in the Peanut Butter, Chocolate-Hazelnut Spread, and Banana Sandwich recipe, a bacon press presses down on a sandwich and gives it a signature flat look. If you don't have a bacon press, use a spatula to press down firmly on the sandwich.

BAKING SHEETS

Baking sheets come in many shapes and sizes. The most common sheets have a ½" rim around all the edges and come in two sizes: half sheets and full sheets. Half sheets are 13" × 18" and full sheets are 26" × 18". Most of the recipes that follow use the half-sheet variety, though quarter sheets are mentioned as well.

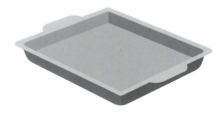

BLENDER

A good-quality, high-powered stand blender helps achieve a smoother consistency in smoothies and dips. Start with a low setting and turn up the speed as larger pieces break up.

BUBBLE WRAP

Bubble Wrap is used in the Honey Bee Cupcakes recipe in order to make a decoration that mimics the look of honeycomb. Use a clean sheet of Bubble Wrap with small bubbles, about ¼" in diameter.

BUNDT PAN

A Bundt pan is a kind of baking pan with a tube down the center to assist with more even baking. A standard size 12-cup pan is best for the recipes in this book.

CAKE PANS

Standard 9" circle and square metal cake pans will help you create cakes and other delicious dishes. Typically, you line these pans with parchment paper to prevent sticking.

COCKTAIL SHAKER

A cocktail shaker makes mixing easy for single-serve mixed drinks, especially if a thicker syrup is used in the recipe. You can also quickly chill a drink during mixing by adding ice to the shaker before shaking. Most standard shakers hold 24 ounces. If you don't have a cocktail shaker, just whisk the mixture well in a large glass or small bowl and strain through a sieve.

COFFEE SUBSTITUTE

Some people are not partial to coffee or might want to enjoy a coffee-style beverage later in the day without caffeine. Many coffee-substitute products that provide a natural caffeine-free experience are available at stores and online retailers. Most are made from malted barley, chicory, and rye. Pero and Caf-Lib are great choices, as they don't require a coffee machine to brew. Simply follow the instructions on the packaging, then add to the recipe in place of cold brew in the Cold Brew Black Caf recipe.

COOLING RACK

A common wire cooling/drying rack is sufficient for the recipes in this book. They are typically made from stainless steel and have straight lines or a crosshatch pattern.

EGG RING

An egg ring is used for the Breakfast Sandwich recipe. This is a silicone or metal mold you place in a nonstick pan to cook eggs in a round shape so they are easier to eat in a sandwich. The standard size is around 3.5" in diameter. If you don't have an egg ring, prepare your eggs like an omelet and fold to fit onto the bun.

ELECTRIC CREPE PAN

An electric crepe pan is suggested in the recipes for crepes and galettes in this book. They provide consistent heat across the cooking surface and typically allow a larger crepe to be made than what can be made in a standard nonstick pan on the stovetop. However, while convenient, an electric crepe pan is not necessary to make crepes or galettes; a large nonstick pan on the stovetop works just fine.

ELECTRIC PRESSURE COOKER

Many different brands are available, but any dependable brand electric pressure cooker will do. Make sure that there is a properly sized inner pot placed in the cooker and that you are careful to avoid steam burns when you release pressure. Electric pressure cookers can save a lot of time in the kitchen and provide a delicious product.

FOOD COLORING

Many of the recipes in this book use food coloring to create the original look found in the Parks. Gel colors are always preferred for solid foods, and liquid colors for drinks. Gel colors have a brighter pop of color than liquid food coloring, and the denser consistency won't change the texture of the dish. If your gel colors come in pots and cannot "drop," use a wooden toothpick to dip into the gel and swipe it through the food you want to color. Repeat for each drop needed.

FOOD PROCESSOR

Food processors are basically high-powered blenders that specialize in chopping dry foods. If you don't have a food processor, a blender will work fine. If you have neither, chopping very finely with a knife works too—it is just more labor intensive, and the pieces will be less uniform.

GLASS PAN

Several recipes in this book use 8" × 8" glass pans. A metal pan can be substituted. Just be sure to check the food more often to prevent overcooking.

GRILL OR GRILL PAN

For items in the following recipes that need to be grilled, an outdoor grill and indoor grill pan are interchangeable for searing food items. Propane grills should be preheated to ensure even cooking. Indoor grill pans need to be greased with cooking oil before use to help prevent sticking. Charcoal grills can also be used. Refer to your grill instructions for safe cooking guidelines.

ICE CREAM MACHINE

The easiest ice cream machines are the ones with a freezable "bowl." This bowl is removed from the freezer right before use, and cream or drink mix is poured directly into the frozen bowl. The bowl then spins on a base, and a paddle mixes and scrapes the inside. Other options are available if you are unable to use this type of ice cream machine. For example, you can use an ice cream bucket–type machine. Pour the mixture from the recipe into the metal inner container and fill the outer bucket with ice and rock salt. Run the machine until the consistency matches the recipe description. Truly, any machine you have is fine.

IMMERSION BLENDER

This kind of blender is convenient because you can leave your soup or sauce in the pot on the stove and purée it without moving to a stand blender or food processor. If you don't have one, however, a stand blender or food processor can work just as well.

MASON JARS

Some jars are called for in this book for pickling or storing foods. Depending on the recipe, you'll be asked to use a pint- or a quart-sized jar. If you don't have any jars on hand, feel free to use any container that is roughly the same size and has a lid.

MEAT TENDERIZER

A meat tenderizer is called for to pat down the chicken in the Not So Little Chicken Sandwich recipe. A standard meat tenderizer is a mallet with a smooth side and a spiky side. Use the spiky side to smash the chicken flat. If you don't have a meat tenderizer, use the bottom of a frying pan to smash the chicken—just be sure to clean the pan well after you're done.

MINI LOAF PAN

Used for the Berry Short Cake recipe, this pan is 6" × 3.5" × 2" and either metal or glass. Your pan doesn't have to be these exact dimensions, but the cooking time in the recipe is formulated for this size.

MOLDS

Some recipes require the use of molds. Silicone or plastic molds will work just fine; just make sure plastic ones are rated to withstand the temperatures of hot candy and won't melt when poured into. A long silicone mold is needed for the Celestial-Sized Candy Bar: Choco-Smash CANDY Bar. You can purchase one from an online retailer. The proper size has mold cavities about 1.5" × 4.5" × 1", which is about the size of a standard candy bar.

MUFFIN PANS

The common muffin pan has twelve divots. Generously grease the pan with cooking oil to prevent sticking.

PARCHMENT PAPER

Almost every recipe in this book that requires baking will instruct you to line the baking sheet or pan with parchment paper. This quick step ensures a more even baking surface and more consistent browning, and greatly reduces the likelihood of your food sticking to the pan. Parchment paper can be found in any grocery store, or online.

PASTRY CUTTER

A pastry cutter is used in The Sword in the Sweet. It is a tool for cutting cold butter into small bits. If you don't have one, you can easily use one or two butter knives instead to cut the butter into bits.

PIPETTE

A pipette is called for in the Proton Punch recipe. The pipette is filled with grenadine and added to the drink as a cute, science-y touch on theme with Pym Test Kitchen. While it does lend a striking look to the drink, a pipette is not necessary, and the grenadine can be added directly to the cup while preparing. Pipettes can easily be found cheaply in bulk from online retailers.

PIPING BAGS

Many recipes in this book use piping bags, but you don't have to go out and buy a fancy set. A heavy-duty plastic sandwich or gallon bag will do nicely. Simply scoop the mixture into the bag, then snip a small edge off one of the bottom corners. Start your hole out small and make it bigger as needed.

PIPING BAG TIPS

Some recipes will call for special piping bag tips. While you don't *need* to use a tip for any recipe in this book, it can make for an eye-catching design.

POTATO MASHER

A potato masher is excellent for not only mashing potatoes, but also crushing berries in a syrup, or any other smashing needs. If you don't have a potato masher, a fork or whisk can be substituted.

POTS AND PANS

Heavy-bottomed saucepans are preferred in many of the following recipes. The thick metal bottom regulates the temperature better and prevents burning. If you don't have heavy-bottomed pans, any appropriately sized pot or pan will do; just keep an extra close eye on foods cooking on the stove. Stir more frequently to prevent burning. Nonstick pans are not usually necessary, but are helpful in some recipes, such as the crepe recipes. The nonstick surface allows the batter to slide off without sticking. If you don't have a nonstick pan, grease the pan with plenty of nonstick cooking spray or oil before starting.

RAMEKINS

Ramekins are small glass or ceramic bowls that can be baked in the oven. If you don't have designated ramekins, check the bottom of your glass storage containers or cereal bowls to see if they are oven-safe.

ROLLING PIN

Rolling pins come in many shapes and sizes, including those that have handles on the sides, French styles, and the straight cylindrical stye. Any variety you have on hand can be used in the following recipes.

SIEVE/SIFTER

The sieves/sifters described in the following recipes refer to a stainless-steel mesh half-dome strainer. Get one with a medium-fine mesh.

SKEWERS

Skewers are a great way to roast meats or vegetables on a grill without allowing them to slip between the grates. Wooden or metal skewers can be used, but be sure to soak wooden skewers in water for at least 30 minutes before using to avoid the wood burning.

STAND MIXER

Almost every recipe in this book that requires mixing uses a stand mixer. This machine makes mixing, whipping, and kneading easy and uniform. If you don't have a stand mixer, the second-best option is a hand mixer. These often also have interchangeable attachments for mixing or whipping. If you have neither, of course you can mix, whip, and knead by hand.

SYRUPS

Syrups are a key part of making many mixed drinks in the Disney Parks. Walt Disney World Resort typically uses the brand Monin for its drinks instead of house-made syrups. This provides consistency and high quality across the resort and is especially useful when drinks change locations—which they often do. If you can't find Monin syrups, other brands work just as well.

THERMOMETERS

A confection or candy thermometer is essential for any candy making or deep-frying. Bringing mixtures to the correct temperature determines the final product's texture and taste. A meat thermometer is crucial to ensure meat is cooked to a safe temperature. Both types of thermometers can be bought at most grocery and big-box stores, or online.

WOK

A wok is a special frying pan that has high walls and narrows as you reach the center. It is particularly useful in making coated meat dishes or stir-fries. If you don't have a wok, any large frying pan will do.

GETTING STARTED

With a deeper understanding of the culinary experiences Disney offers, and a kitchen stocked with the tools you'll want for making the recipes in Part 2, it's time for that delicious next step: cooking! Take each recipe one at a time and don't be afraid to experiment with flavors and designs to tailor these Disney originals to you and your tastes. If you're unsure about something, just refer back to this chapter!

····· PART 2 ·····

Disney Parks Restaurant Recipes

You're ready to get cooking! The following chapters hold the secrets to some of the most popular and most iconic Disney restaurant foods and beverages. These recipes have the power to take you and your family and friends to destinations as familiar as the dining room of your favorite animated movie or as mysterious as other galaxies. What you make will steer your adventures!

The chapters in this part are organized by cuisine type: Breakfast, Lunch, Appetizers and Snacks, Main Dishes, Desserts, and Drinks. But don't feel confined to serve any of these at a certain time of day. Anything goes in your own kitchen! Whatever you choose to make, get excited because you are now initiated as an unofficial Disney chef!

CHAPTER 3

Breakfast

Nothing kick-starts a busy schedule (or a relaxing weekend at home) like a satisfying and delicious breakfast. The recipes in this chapter will allow you to begin your day with a little magic!

Some of these dishes are perfect for a quick meal, like the Breakfast Sandwich, American Breakfast Burrito, or Slow-Roasted Ham, Swiss & Egg Croissant. Others are better for a chill morning at home, like the Caramel Monkey Bread or Melba Crêpes. Whatever kind of pick-me-up you are looking for, this chapter has it! And not only are these delicious breakfast options, but each comes with a little pixie dust since they originate from the happiest and most magical places on Earth. So throw off your sheets, rub the sleep out of your eyes, and get to the kitchen: Breakfast awaits!

American Breakfast Burrito

••••• **Galactic Grill, Disneyland** •••••

Diners in California have been stuffing French fries in burritos since at least the 1980s, and customers line up to get them. As a riff on this concept, Disneyland has added hash brown patties to these burritos for that same starchy potato goodness, but tailored for the morning. Hash brown patties can be found at your local grocery store near the frozen French fries.

SERVES 1

- ½ tablespoon salted butter
- 2 large eggs
- 1 tablespoon sour cream
- ½ teaspoon salt
- ¼ teaspoon ground black pepper
- 1 (10") flour tortilla
- ½ cup shredded sharp Cheddar cheese
- 2 (1–2-ounce) precooked breakfast sausage patties, warmed
- 1 frozen hash brown patty, warmed
- 2 strips cooked bacon
- 1 tablespoon chopped green onions

1. In a large nonstick skillet over medium heat, add butter and allow to melt. Add eggs and sour cream and stir and scramble until cooked through, about 3 minutes. Sprinkle with salt and pepper and scoop into a bowl. Wipe out skillet.
2. In same skillet over medium heat, add tortilla. Place prepared eggs on tortilla and sprinkle with cheese, then place sausage patties, hash brown patty, bacon, and green onions on top. Fold tortilla over fillings into a tight burrito and flip to grill opposite side 1–2 minutes until browned. Transfer to a plate and enjoy immediately.

Disney Parks Tip

At Galactic Grill, located adjacent to Buzz Lightyear Astro Blasters in Tomorrowland, you may catch a lightsaber training or Darth Vader himself on the Tomorrowland Terrace stage while enjoying your meal!

Mustafarian Lava Rolls

..... **Oga's Cantina at Disneyland and Disney's Hollywood Studios** .....

Mustafar was once just your run-of-the-mill lava-covered factory planet but is now famous as the location Anakin Skywalker (spoiler alert) became Darth Vader and set up his base. Whether or not Darth Vader wakes up with a Mustafarian Lava Roll is unknown, but you can still feel like the Supreme Commander of your kitchen with this explosive flavor combination of chocolate sandwich cookies and strawberry glaze.

SERVES 5

- 1 (5-count) refrigerated can large cinnamon rolls
- ¼ cup strawberry glaze
- 5 chocolate sandwich cookies

1. Bake cinnamon rolls according to package instructions, then place each on its own plate.
2. Drizzle each cinnamon roll with 1–2 tablespoons strawberry glaze.
3. Pull apart chocolate sandwich cookies and crush chocolate cookies into fine crumbs in a small bowl. Crumble white interiors into a separate small bowl. Sprinkle chocolate crumbs across cinnamon rolls and top with white crumbles. Serve immediately.

Mix It Up!

There are lots of flavors of glaze toppings available at the grocery store; try using a different flavor each time you make these. You can also use different cookie crumbles!

Breakfast Sandwich

······ **Carnation Café, Disneyland** ······

Nothing starts the day off better than a big ol' breakfast sandwich. The key to making this sandwich shine is twofold: incredibly fluffy and buttery bread, and thick-sliced bacon. These two elements elevate this sandwich from a drive-through staple to the highlight of your day! Carnation Café has been a Main Street, U.S.A., institution since opening day in 1955 and continues to delight Disneyland guests, especially with its breakfast options. Serve this sandwich with orange slices and breakfast potatoes.

SERVES 1

- 1 large egg
- 1 tablespoon shredded provolone cheese
- 1 tablespoon shredded Swiss cheese
- 1 tablespoon shredded sharp Cheddar cheese
- ½ teaspoon salt
- ¼ teaspoon ground black pepper
- 2 tablespoons water
- 1 brioche bun, sliced open
- 4 thick strips applewood-smoked bacon
- 1 thin slice sharp Cheddar cheese

1. In a medium nonstick pan over medium heat, place an egg ring, then grease ring with nonstick cooking spray. Crack egg into ring and gently break yolk with a fork.
2. Add shredded cheeses, salt, and pepper on egg and swirl using a utensil to incorporate. Pour water into pan and cover with a lid. Allow to steam 3 minutes or until egg is completely cooked through. Remove egg ring with tongs or a pot holder.
3. Assemble sandwich with bottom brioche bun, bacon, egg round, Cheddar cheese slice, and top bun. Serve immediately.

Sausage and Gravy Tots

••••• **The Friar's Nook, Magic Kingdom** •••••

For breakfast, gravy is most commonly slathered over biscuits, but at The Friar's Nook, they decided to use potato tots as a base instead! And aren't we glad they did? The crispy potatoes and the savory gravy make a perfect pairing. The Friar's Nook seating area can get a lot of sun exposure in the morning, so if you're trying this recipe in the Park, be sure to grab a table in the shade while you wait for your food.

SERVES 6

1 pound ground breakfast sausage
¼ cup all-purpose flour
2 cups heavy whipping cream
1 cup whole milk
1 tablespoon plus 1 teaspoon ground black pepper, divided
2 teaspoons salt, divided
1 tablespoon salted butter
6 large eggs
2 tablespoons sour cream
6 cups frozen potato tots, prepared

1. In a large skillet over medium heat, brown sausage until no longer pink, 5–7 minutes. Sprinkle with flour and stir 2 minutes to combine. Slowly stir in whipping cream and milk, followed by 1 tablespoon pepper and 1 teaspoon salt. Reduce heat to low and simmer 5 minutes or until gravy has thickened.
2. Place a medium nonstick skillet over medium heat and add butter. Crack eggs into a medium bowl and add sour cream, remaining 1 teaspoon pepper, and remaining 1 teaspoon salt. Whisk until well combined, about 2 minutes. Pour into preheated skillet and scramble until cooked through, 3–5 minutes.
3. Assemble six serving bowls each with 1 cup prepared tots, a scoop of scrambled eggs, and a scoop of sausage gravy. Serve immediately.

Mix It Up!

You know what are like potato tots? French fries! Just cook a batch of frozen French fries and top with these ingredients for a similar quick dish.

Cinnamon Rolls

······ **Jolly Holiday Bakery Cafe, Disneyland** ······

This recipe is sure to set you up for a supercalifragilisticexpialidocious day! Although it does contain a fair bit more than just one spoonful of sugar, who's counting when you're at Disney? Make these at home for a special occasion or a fun-filled Saturday. The smothering of icing and dusting of cinnamon allow these to shine.

SERVES 12

For Dough
½ cup salted butter, melted
1½ cups whole milk
6½ cups plus 1 tablespoon all-purpose flour, divided
2 (0.25-ounce) packets dry active yeast
½ cup granulated sugar
1 teaspoon salt
½ cup room-temperature water
2 large eggs

For Filling
2 cups light brown sugar
2 tablespoons ground cinnamon
1 cup salted butter, softened

1. Grease a 9" × 13" pan with nonstick cooking spray and set aside.
2. To make Dough: In a medium bowl, combine melted butter and milk.
3. In the bowl of a stand mixer fitted with paddle attachment, add 2½ cups flour, yeast, sugar, and salt. Add water, eggs, and butter mixture. Mix on low speed until well combined, about 2 minutes. Add remaining flour ½ cup at a time while mixing until Dough starts to form a ball.
4. Switch to the dough hook attachment and knead Dough on low speed 5 minutes.
5. Remove Dough from bowl, sprinkle 1 tablespoon flour in bowl, and place Dough back in the same bowl. Cover with a clean kitchen towel and let rise 10 minutes in a warm place.
6. To make Filling: In a medium bowl, mix all ingredients until well combined. Set aside.

For Cream Cheese Icing

8 ounces cream cheese, softened

¼ cup salted butter, softened

2 cups confectioners' sugar

1 teaspoon vanilla extract

½ cup heavy cream

⅛ teaspoon salt

For Assembly

2 teaspoons ground cinnamon

7. Roll out Dough into a long rectangle, about 3' × 2'. Spread Filling evenly across the whole surface of the Dough. Starting at a long end, roll Dough like a jelly roll. Cut the roll into twelve equal-sized cinnamon rolls and place them (swirl side down) in prepared pan. If they don't all fit in one pan, place extras in a second greased pan. Allow to rise 30 minutes in a warm place.
8. Preheat oven to 375°F. Bake rolls 20–30 minutes until browned and cooked through.
9. To make Cream Cheese Icing: In a medium saucepan over medium heat, add all ingredients. Whisk to combine and cook about 5 minutes or until all ingredients are combined and melty. Remove from heat.
10. To Assemble: Place each roll on its own plate. Smother with Cream Cheese Icing and finish with a light dusting of cinnamon. Serve.

Mickey-Shaped Pancakes

Red Rose Taverne, Disneyland

Mickey-Shaped Pancakes have been served across the Disney Parks since forever, but they have migrated from one dining location to the next. In the 1990 classic *Disney Sing-Along-Songs: Disneyland Fun*, hungry kids chow down on these very same pancakes while singing "Rumbly in My Tumbly" with Winnie the Pooh. They're easy to make at home, so you don't need to wait for a special occasion to break out this recipe! Serve with a side of bacon or sausage.

SERVES 4

- 2 cups all-purpose flour
- 3 tablespoons granulated sugar
- 1¼ teaspoons baking powder
- 1¼ teaspoons baking soda
- 1¼ teaspoons salt
- 2 large eggs, beaten
- 1 cup buttermilk
- ¼ cup lemon-lime soda
- ¾ cup water
- 1 teaspoon vanilla extract
- 3 tablespoons salted butter, melted
- 4 tablespoons salted butter, divided
- 1 tablespoon confectioners' sugar
- 1 cup mixed berry jam

1. In a large bowl, whisk together flour, granulated sugar, baking powder, baking soda, and salt. Add in eggs, buttermilk, lemon-lime soda, water, vanilla, and melted butter. Stir to combine.
2. Heat a large nonstick skillet over medium heat. Melt 1 tablespoon butter in hot pan. Scoop ¼ cup batter into middle of pan and add 2 tablespoons batter to each side of the top of the first circle, to make Mickey ears. Cook 1–2 minutes until bottom is golden brown, then carefully flip entire "Mickey." Cook an additional 1–2 minutes until entire pancake is cooked through. Transfer to a plate and repeat with remaining 3 tablespoons butter and batter.
3. Sprinkle pancakes with confectioners' sugar and serve with berry jam on the side.

Cinnamon-Sugar Doughnuts

***** **The Friar's Nook, Magic Kingdom** *****

These portable and bite-sized doughnut holes are perfect to pass around to all your kids or friends while running from one ride to the next. When making them at home, you might want to multiply the recipe because everyone is going to want three or four or five! If you want to get fancy, add a drizzle of chocolate, caramel, or strawberry topping; in your kitchen, you can enjoy them however you like!

SERVES 2

For Doughnut Holes
- 48 ounces vegetable oil, for frying
- 2 cups all-purpose flour plus extra for dusting
- 3 tablespoons granulated sugar
- 1 tablespoon baking powder
- 1 teaspoon salt
- ¼ cup cold salted butter, cubed
- ¾ cup whole milk

For Topping
- ½ cup granulated sugar
- 2 teaspoons ground cinnamon

1. To make Doughnut Holes: In a large saucepan over medium heat, preheat oil to 350°F.
2. In a food processor, add 2 cups flour, sugar, baking powder, and salt. Pulse five times to combine. Continue to pulse while adding in cold butter cubes one at a time. Mixture should resemble coarse crumbs. Continue to pulse while adding in milk until dough comes together in a ball.
3. Transfer dough from food processor to a lightly floured surface and knead with your hands 3–5 minutes until dough is no longer sticky. Add more flour, 1 tablespoon at a time, if necessary.
4. Line a plate with paper towels. Divide dough into twelve (1½") balls. Once oil is heated, carefully add half the balls to the hot oil and stir occasionally while frying 3–5 minutes until balls are golden brown and cooked through. Transfer to prepared plate and repeat with remaining balls.
5. To make Topping: In a shallow dish, combine sugar and cinnamon. Roll hot balls in cinnamon and sugar (save or discard excess cinnamon sugar) and then serve.

Classique Galettes

La Crêperie de Paris, EPCOT

A savory ham and cheese crepe for breakfast? Yum! In fact, there is no limit to what time of day you can enjoy these galettes—breakfast, lunch, dinner, or snack time, they will hit the spot. Hearty buckwheat adds depth of flavor to the crepe base, and creamy cheese and sweet ham make this a *délicieux* dish.

SERVES 6

For Crepes
- 1 cup buckwheat flour
- 2 large eggs
- ½ cup whole milk
- ½ teaspoon salt
- 2 tablespoons salted butter, melted

For Assembly
- 6 tablespoons salted butter, divided
- 6 large eggs
- 1 teaspoon salt
- 1 teaspoon ground black pepper
- ½ cup grated Swiss cheese
- 6 slices deli ham

1. To make Crepes: Add all ingredients to a blender and pulse until well combined, about 1 minute.
2. Heat an electric crepe pan or a large skillet to medium-high heat and spray pan with nonstick cooking spray. Pouring directly from blender, swirl about ¼–½ cup batter in pan to evenly coat the bottom. Cook about 2 minutes, then slide a spatula around outside edges and flip to cook opposite side 2 minutes more. Transfer Crepe to a large plate and repeat with remaining batter, spraying pan with nonstick cooking spray between each batch. Excess batter and cooked Crepes can be kept covered in the refrigerator up to 1 week.
3. To Assemble: Heat a large skillet over medium heat and melt ½ tablespoon butter. Crack 1 egg in the center of skillet and cook 2–3 minutes until whites have set and yolk is still runny. Sprinkle with a little salt and pepper and set aside. Repeat with remaining eggs, salt, and pepper.
4. Wipe out skillet and add ½ tablespoon butter. Once melted, place 1 cooked Crepe in pan and sprinkle a thin layer of Swiss cheese in the center of Crepe. Add 1 ham slice and 1 cooked egg. Fold in the edges of Crepe to form a square, and immediately transfer Crepe to a plate. Repeat with remaining butter, Crepes, cooked eggs, and ham to make six total galettes, then serve.

Melba Crêpes

⋯⋯• La Crêperie de Paris, EPCOT •⋯⋯

In 1892, Nellie Melba from Australia performed as the lead in the opera *Lohengrin*. To show how much he loved it, the Duke of Orléans commissioned the famous French chef Escoffier to make a dessert in her honor. As La Crêperie de Paris celebrates French cuisine, honoring the great Chef Escoffier with this dish fits perfectly on theme.

SERVES 4

For Red Berries Sauce
1 cup frozen raspberries
1 cup frozen strawberries
1 cup granulated sugar
1 tablespoon lemon juice

For Crepes
1 cup all-purpose flour
2 large eggs
½ cup whole milk
½ teaspoon salt
2 tablespoons salted butter, melted

For Assembly
1 cup fresh blackberries
2 large peaches, peeled, pitted, and sliced
4 tablespoons sliced almonds

1. To make Red Berries Sauce: In a small saucepan over medium heat, add all ingredients and stir to combine. Continue to stir and mash berries with a potato masher until mixture comes to a boil, about 5 minutes.
2. Remove from heat and strain though a medium-mesh sieve into a small bowl, discarding solids. Place in refrigerator 30 minutes to cool.
3. To make Crepes: Add all ingredients to a blender and pulse until well combined, about 1 minute.
4. Preheat an electric crepe pan or a large skillet to medium-high heat and spray pan with nonstick cooking spray. Pouring directly from blender, swirl about ¼–½ cup batter in pan to evenly coat the bottom. Cook about 2 minutes, then slide a spatula around outside edges and flip to cook opposite side 2 minutes more. Transfer Crepe to a large plate and repeat with remaining batter, spraying pan with nonstick cooking spray after making each Crepe. Excess batter or cooked Crepes can be kept covered in the refrigerator up to 1 week.
5. To Assemble: Lay 1 Crêpe on a large plate. Add ¼ cup blackberries and a handful of peach slices in the center of Crepe. Fold in the edges of Crepe to form a square. Drizzle with Red Berries Sauce and sprinkle with 1 tablespoon almonds. Repeat with remaining Crepes, blackberries, peaches, Red Berries Sauce, and almonds. Serve immediately.

Breakfast Bowls

Woody's Lunch Box, Disney's Hollywood Studios

Have you ever heard of Hawaiian Haystacks? It is a rice and chicken dish that basically starts with a scoop of rice, and everyone can add their choice of ingredients to their "haystack." This recipe has a similar vibe: a base of potato tots piled high with breakfast favorites. Line up ingredients on the counter, and family or friends can choose exactly what to stack up in their bowl.

SERVES 6

- 1 pound smoked beef brisket, finely diced
- ¼ cup all-purpose flour
- 2 cups heavy whipping cream
- 1 cup whole milk
- 2 teaspoons salt, divided
- 2 teaspoons ground black pepper, divided
- 1 tablespoon salted butter
- 6 large eggs
- 2 tablespoons sour cream
- ½ teaspoon smoked paprika
- 6 cups frozen potato tots, prepared
- ¼ cup diced green onions

1. In a large skillet over medium heat, warm up brisket 2 minutes. Sprinkle with flour and stir 2 minutes to combine. Slowly stir in whipping cream and milk, followed by 1 teaspoon salt and 1 teaspoon pepper. Reduce heat to low and simmer 5 minutes or until gravy has thickened.
2. Place a medium nonstick skillet over medium heat and add butter. Crack eggs into a medium bowl and add sour cream, paprika, remaining 1 teaspoon salt, and remaining 1 teaspoon pepper. Whisk until well combined, about 2 minutes. Pour into preheated skillet and scramble until cooked through, 3–5 minutes.
3. Assemble each of six bowls with 1 cup prepared tots, followed by a scoop of scrambled eggs and a scoop of gravy. Top with green onions and serve immediately.

Warm Glazed Doughnut

••••• Sci-Fi Dine-In Theater Restaurant, Disney's Hollywood Studios •••••

Sci-Fi Dine-In Theater Restaurant is a playful eatery at Disney's Hollywood Studios that mimics the feeling of going to the drive-in theater on a summer evening. Clips from classic flicks are shown on the big screen, and the tables are designed to look like cars! Since breakfast isn't served at Sci-Fi, this dish comes and goes from the dessert menu. But you can enjoy it any time the mood for a doughnut and ice cream hits! This recipe is simple because you don't need to reinvent the wheel: All these ingredients are easily accessible at the grocery store and can be assembled quickly for a yummy treat.

SERVES 1

1 glazed doughnut
1 cup apple pie filling
1 teaspoon ground cinnamon
½ cup vanilla bean ice cream
1 tablespoon caramel sauce

1. In a shallow microwave-safe bowl, add glazed doughnut and heat in microwave 30 seconds. Set aside.
2. In a small microwave-safe bowl, add apple pie filling and cinnamon. Stir to combine and microwave 30 seconds.
3. Scoop cinnamon-spiced apple pie filling into bowl with doughnut. Scoop ice cream on top of doughnut and drizzle with caramel sauce. Serve immediately.

Marshall's Favorite Sausage, Egg, and Cheese Biscuits

••••• **Pongu Pongu, Disney's Animal Kingdom** •••••

Marshall Lamm is a character featured at Disney's Animal Kingdom who founded Alpha Centauri Expeditions (ACE) and paved the way for tourism and more frequent travel to Pandora. He also invented a Na'vi language translation device that helps humans and Na'vi communicate with one another. In his honor, Pongu Pongu serves his favorite sandwich so that all humans visiting Pandora can start their day the Marshall way!

SERVES 8

For Biscuits
- 2 cups all-purpose flour plus extra for dusting
- 2 tablespoons baking powder
- 2 tablespoons granulated sugar
- 1 teaspoon salt
- ⅓ cup cold salted butter, cut into pieces
- 1 cup whole milk

For Eggs
- 16 large eggs
- 1 teaspoon salt
- 1 teaspoon ground black pepper
- 2 cups shredded Cheddar cheese

1. To make Biscuits: Line a baking sheet with parchment paper and set aside.
2. In a food processor, add 2 cups flour, baking powder, sugar, and salt. Pulse a few times to combine. Add in butter pieces one at a time and continue to pulse until mixture resembles coarse crumbs. Slowly pour milk into food processor while continuing to pulse until well combined.
3. Thoroughly dust a countertop with flour and turn dough out onto flour. Cover with a towel and allow to rest 30 minutes.
4. Preheat oven to 425°F. Remove towel and dust top of dough with flour. Roll gently using a rolling pin until it forms about a 10" × 6" rectangle. Use a generously floured biscuit cutter or glass about 3" in diameter as a cutter for the Biscuits. Press the cutter or cup straight down without twisting to avoid pinching the dough.

For Assembly

8 cooked sausage patties, warmed

5. Place cut Biscuits on prepared baking sheet and bake 10–15 minutes until Biscuits have risen and are golden brown. Remove from oven.
6. To make Eggs: Place a medium nonstick pan over medium heat and grease with nonstick cooking spray. Crack 2 eggs in a small bowl and whisk to incorporate yolks and whites. Add $\frac{1}{8}$ teaspoon salt and $\frac{1}{8}$ teaspoon pepper. Fold in $\frac{1}{4}$ cup shredded cheese. Pour egg mixture into preheated pan and cover with a lid. Allow to cook 2 minutes, then flip, cover, and cook 2 minutes more or until egg mixture is cooked through. Remove from pan and fold into a square. Repeat with remaining eggs, seasonings, and cheese.
7. To Assemble: Cut 1 Biscuit in half sideways and place 1 sausage patty and 1 egg and cheese square on one half. Top with second Biscuit half. Repeat with remaining Biscuits, sausage, and Eggs and serve immediately.

Avocado Toast

···•• **Pacific Wharf Café, Disney California Adventure** ••···

Creamy avocado and crunchy toast is a pairing made in heaven, and this version takes it a step further with juicy roasted tomatoes, balsamic glaze, and cilantro. Pair this toast with a cup of Cold Brew Black Caf (see recipe in Chapter 8). This breakfast combination would be hard to accomplish at Disney Parks since Pacific Wharf Café and Docking Bay 7 Food and Cargo are nowhere near each other (and this Avocado Toast has been known to duck in and out of the Pacific Wharf Café menu), but the magic can happen in your kitchen!

SERVES 1

- 1 medium ripe avocado, peeled, pitted, and mashed
- 1 slice sourdough bread, toasted
- 5 cherry tomatoes
- 3 balls mini mozzarella cheese
- 1 tablespoon balsamic glaze
- 1 sprig fresh cilantro, chopped
- ¼ teaspoon flake salt
- ⅛ teaspoon ground black pepper

1. Smear mashed avocado over toasted bread slice.
2. Spear cherry tomatoes on a skewer or long fork and place into direct flame of a gas grill or stovetop about 1 minute to blacken skin.
3. Place tomatoes on avocado, then place mozzarella balls on top. Drizzle with balsamic glaze, top with cilantro, and sprinkle with salt and pepper. Serve immediately.

Ever-Expanding Cinna-Pym Toast

Pym Test Kitchen, Disney California Adventure

One of the most unique aspects of the food served at Pym Test Kitchen is the presentation. The Ever-Expanding Cinna-Pym Toast is served on a pizza pan with graph paper laid down under the food. It almost feels like you are about to tuck into a science experiment! At Pym's, two strips of bacon are placed on top of the toast, and it is served with an adorable sunny-side-up quail egg and mandarin orange slice on the side.

SERVES 4

- 1 large loaf French bread, cut into ½" square pieces
- 2 tablespoons blue straight sprinkles
- 6 large eggs
- ¼ cup salted butter, melted
- 2 cups half-and-half
- 2 teaspoons ground cinnamon
- 1 tablespoon vanilla extract
- 1 cup pure maple syrup

1. Cover a quarter sheet pan with parchment paper. Place bread squares and sprinkles on sheet and toss to combine.
2. In a medium bowl, add eggs, butter, half-and-half, cinnamon, and vanilla. Whisk 2 minutes or until well combined. Pour mixture over bread and gently fold with spatula to ensure all bread is wet. Cover with plastic wrap and refrigerate 6 hours or overnight.
3. Preheat oven to 375°F. Remove pan from refrigerator and bake 30–40 minutes until egg is cooked through. Remove from oven and allow to cool 10 minutes.
4. Cut into four long strips and serve each strip with ¼ cup maple syrup.

Slow-Roasted Ham, Swiss & Egg Croissants

The Trolley Car Café, Disney's Hollywood Studios

If this sandwich sounds familiar, it's because The Trolley Car Café at Disney's Hollywood Studios is actually a Starbucks location! Many of the Disney Parks host Starbucks shops and sell the company's coffees, sandwiches, and pastries. A Slow-Roasted Ham, Swiss & Egg Croissant is great paired with your favorite cup of joe.

SERVES 8

- 1 (8-ounce) can refrigerated crescent rolls
- 8 large eggs
- 1 teaspoon salt
- 1 teaspoon ground black pepper
- 16 thin slices slow-roasted deli ham
- 8 slices Swiss cheese

1. Preheat oven to 375°F. Grease a muffin tin with nonstick cooking spray.
2. Lay out crescent roll dough sheet flat. Cut entire sheet in half lengthwise and then widthwise on horizontal perforations. Pinch together diagonal perforations and make one long lengthwise cut across remaining pieces to finish with eight long, skinny rectangles. Roll each rectangle up into a tight scroll and place 1 roll into each muffin divot. Use a greased cup to firmly press each roll down into the divot.
3. Bake 9–12 minutes until golden brown. Remove from oven and allow to cool 10 minutes in pan.
4. Grease a small skillet and egg ring generously with nonstick cooking spray and place over medium-high heat. Crack 1 egg into egg ring, pop yolk with a fork, and sprinkle with ⅛ teaspoon salt and ⅛ teaspoon pepper. Cover skillet and cook 2 minutes. Remove ring, flip egg, and cook an additional 2 minutes or until cooked through.
5. Place 2 ham slices and 1 cheese slice on egg, cover, and allow cheese to melt about 2 minutes. Remove from pan and repeat with remaining ingredients.
6. Slice each crescent bun in half sideways and place 1 egg, ham, and cheese stack on the bottom crescent piece, then top with the top crescent pieces. Serve immediately.

Caramel Monkey Bread

······ **Hollywood & Vine, Disney's Hollywood Studios** ······

Roll out the red carpet for this showstopper of a breakfast! Easy to put together and an absolute crowd-pleaser, Caramel Monkey Bread might end up on your menu every Saturday morning. At Hollywood & Vine, Disney characters are often seen cruising and schmoozing among the tables. Depending on the theme of the meal, characters may be Minnie Mouse and her friends, or stars of your favorite Disney Junior shows, like Doc McStuffins or Fancy Nancy!

SERVES 6

- ½ cup granulated sugar
- 1 teaspoon ground cinnamon
- 2 (12-ounce) cans refrigerated biscuits, each biscuit cut into quarters
- ½ cup salted butter, melted
- ¾ cup light brown sugar

1. Preheat oven to 350°F. Grease a Bundt pan with nonstick cooking spray and set aside.
2. In a large zip-top bag, add granulated sugar and cinnamon and shake to combine. Drop biscuit quarters one at a time into bag of cinnamon sugar. Seal bag and shake to coat biscuit pieces. Use tongs to pluck sugared biscuit pieces out of bag and into prepared pan and evenly distribute.
3. In a small bowl, mix butter and brown sugar, then drizzle over biscuit pieces.
4. Bake 35–45 minutes until biscuits are cooked through and biscuits are no longer wet or doughy in the center. Allow bread to cool in pan 10 minutes, then invert onto a plate and cut into sections to serve.

CHAPTER 4

Lunch

The busiest meal of the day at the Disney Parks is undoubtably lunch. Everyone is hungry and in need of a little pick-me-up to keep energy high until dinnertime. While Disney doesn't usually make a distinction between "lunch" or "dinner" on most menus, the recipes in this chapter are considered "lunch" because they are smaller or lighter bites that can be prepared quicker than most "main dishes." Of course, these "lunch" foods would be yummy any time of day, so you do you!

There are options for every palate, and even the pickiest of eaters will find something to love. Check out the exciting vegetarian options, like the Outback Vegetable Skewers and the Declaration Salad. Or, if you want some meat in your lunch, try the Orange Chicken, Lobster Bisque, or Not So Little Chicken Sandwich. Looking for a sweeter meal? The Peanut Butter, Chocolate-Hazelnut Spread, and Banana Sandwich is a simple twist on the nostalgic favorite. It's time to infuse your midday meal with some creative Disney flavors!

Chieftain Chicken Skewers

..... **Bengal Barbecue, Disneyland** .....

Juicy chicken marinated in sweet Polynesian sauce makes for an excellent lunch (or dinner!). And the leftovers even save well for a delicious meal the next day. Just remove the chicken from the skewers and store in a sealed container or zip-top bag. Reheat and place over rice or in a stir-fry. Or try the chicken chilled and chopped on top of a salad. It will keep in the refrigerator up to one week. Skippers of all ages go ape for these skewers!

YIELDS 18 SKEWERS

- 2 teaspoons minced garlic
- 1 tablespoon red wine vinegar
- 1 cup ketchup
- ½ cup light brown sugar
- ½ cup soy sauce
- ¼ cup pulp-free orange juice concentrate
- ¼ cup canned crushed pineapple
- ¼ cup pineapple juice
- 1 teaspoon ground black pepper
- 2½ pounds boneless skinless chicken breast, cut into strips

1. In a large bowl, combine garlic, vinegar, ketchup, brown sugar, soy sauce, orange juice concentrate, crushed pineapple, pineapple juice, and pepper. Separate out 1 cup sauce, cover, and set aside. Place chicken strips into remaining sauce and stir to coat. Cover and refrigerate both sauce mixtures 6 hours up to overnight.
2. In a large bowl or in the kitchen sink, soak eighteen wooden skewers a minimum of 30 minutes. Preheat a grill pan over medium heat and grease with nonstick cooking spray.
3. Lace marinated chicken strips lengthwise onto wet skewers and place onto preheated grill pan. Pour and brush on 1–2 tablespoons reserved sauce per chicken strip. Working in batches, grill and flip strips until chicken is cooked through to 165°F, about 10 minutes. Remove from heat and serve immediately.

Outback Vegetable Skewers

······ **Bengal Barbecue, Disneyland** ······

Outback Vegetable Skewers are a great vegetarian option if you're looking for a yummy, quick lunch. To make getting lunch at Bengal Barbecue even quicker, try mobile ordering! Simply pull up the menu on your Walt Disney World app and choose which items you'd like and what time you'd like to pick them up. Then skip the line and grab your freshly prepped food!

SERVES 4

- 2 medium red bell peppers, each cut into 8 thick strips
- 1 medium yellow squash, cut lengthwise and into 1" segments
- 1 medium zucchini, cut lengthwise and into 1" segments
- 1 medium red onion, peeled and cut into chunks
- ¼ cup olive oil
- 1 teaspoon salt
- 1 teaspoon ground black pepper
- ½ fresh lemon, cut into 4 slices

1. In a large bowl or the kitchen sink, soak four wooden skewers a minimum of 30 minutes. Preheat a grill pan over medium heat and grease with nonstick cooking spray.
2. In a large bowl, stir together bell pepper, squash, zucchini, and red onion with olive oil, salt, and black pepper.
3. Alternating vegetables, stick onto wet skewers until skewers are full. Working in batches, grill and flip until vegetables are cooked through and slightly charred, about 10 minutes. Serve with lemon wedges on the side.

Cooking Hack

Make your at-home operation even quicker by prepping all your vegetables the day before. Cut them up and place them in individual bags or sealed containers and pop them in the refrigerator. Then just take them out and assemble the skewers when you're ready to cook.

Ronto-Less Garden Wraps

Ronto Roasters, Disneyland and Disney's Hollywood Studios

Although Ronto Roasters is well known across the galaxy for the juiciest and tastiest ronto sausages, it also caters to people hoping to save a ronto or two with a meat-free wrap. And instead of simply swapping out the ronto meat for a meatless variety, this wrap features a whole new cast of flavors. Spicy Kimchi Slaw and gochujang spread provide a kick worthy of smugglers from the Outer Rim. Even if you're not vegetarian, give this wrap a try next time you're in Batuu, or simply looking for a tasty meal at home.

SERVES 2

For Sweet Pickled Cucumbers

- 1 cup granulated sugar
- 1½ cups water
- ½ cup distilled white vinegar
- 2 medium cucumbers, sliced thin
- 1 tablespoon salt

For Spicy Kimchi Slaw

- 8 stalks green onion, white tips trimmed away
- ¼ cup prepared kimchi
- 1 tablespoon kimchi juice (from jar)
- 1 tablespoon rice vinegar
- 1 teaspoon sriracha
- 1 teaspoon sesame oil
- 2 tablespoons vegetable oil
- 2 cups tricolor coleslaw
- 1 cup shredded carrots

1. To make Sweet Picked Cucumbers: In a medium saucepan over medium heat, combine sugar and water and stir occasionally until bubbles start to form around the edges of pan, about 5 minutes.
2. Remove from heat and add in vinegar. Allow to cool to room temperature, about 1 hour.
3. In a medium bowl, toss cucumber slices with salt and let sit 15 minutes. Strain cucumbers and pat dry with paper towels, then place cucumbers in a quart-sized Mason jar. Pour brine liquid over cucumbers, cover, and refrigerate 2 hours up to overnight.
4. To make Spicy Kimchi Slaw: In a blender, add green onion, kimchi, kimchi juice, vinegar, sriracha, and sesame oil. Blend until smooth, about 2 minutes. While continuing to blend, slowly add in vegetable oil in a steady stream and blend until mixture becomes thick, about 2 minutes.

(continued) ▶

For Assembly

2 pita breads

2 tablespoons plant-based gochujang spread

2 plant-based sausages, heated

5. Place tricolor coleslaw and carrots in a medium bowl and mix with desired amount of dressing from blender. Excess can be stored in a sealed plastic container up to 1 week.
6. To Assemble: Place pita breads on two plates. Smear gochujang spread on pita and place 1 plant-based sausage on each pita, followed by a scoop of Spicy Kimchi Slaw and a layer of Sweet Pickled Cucumbers. Serve immediately.

Disney Parks Tip

Next time you're in Batuu, be sure to download and open the "Play Disney Parks" app. This robust system includes fun scavenger hunts and tricky hacks that actually manipulate real items in the Land! For instance, you can bounty hunt for fugitives from the law, or give the Millennium Falcon a quick tune-up. It is sure to keep younglings (and oldlings!) entertained for hours.

Declaration Salad

Liberty Tree Tavern, Magic Kingdom

Liberty Tree Tavern serves a meal similar to a traditional Thanksgiving Day meal... every day of the year! Turkey, mashed potatoes, stuffing, yum! And nothing goes better with a heavy dish than a light, vinegar-based salad. Pair it with any meal for a refreshing bite. Once you finish up eating at Liberty Tree Tavern, look up at the windows in Liberty Square and you may see Muppets chatting with one another!

SERVES 6

- 2 tablespoons apple cider vinegar
- 2 tablespoons Dijon mustard
- 1 small shallot, peeled and quartered
- 2 tablespoons honey
- ½ cup olive oil
- ½ teaspoon salt
- ½ teaspoon ground black pepper
- 6 cups chopped mixed greens lettuce
- ½ medium red onion, peeled and sliced thin
- 1 large carrot, peeled and shredded
- 2 cups cherry tomatoes

1. In a food processor or blender, add apple cider vinegar, Dijon mustard, shallot, honey, olive oil, salt, and pepper. Pulse about five times until shallot is chopped and ingredients are combined.
2. In a large serving bowl, add lettuce, red onion, carrot, and cherry tomatoes. Drizzle on desired amount of dressing and toss to coat. Serve. Leftover dressing can be kept in a sealed container in the refrigerator up to 1 week.

The Sun Bonnet Trio Strawberry Salad

Pecos Bill Tall Tale Inn and Cafe, Magic Kingdom

The Sun Bonnet Trio is the adorable girl group (Bunny, Bubbles, and Beulah) from the Country Bear Jamboree who sing the crowd favorite "All the Guys Who Turn Me On Turn Me Down." This salad is a tribute to them and is a Fiftieth Anniversary of Walt Disney World specialty item. Whether you love The Sun Bonnet Trio or this is the first time you've heard of the group, this salad will be a huge hit for anyone looking for a bright and light summer salad.

SERVES 6

For Creamy Strawberry Dressing
- 1 cup hulled fresh strawberries
- 2 tablespoons apple cider vinegar
- 2 tablespoons light brown sugar
- ¼ cup olive oil
- 1 teaspoon lemon juice

For Assembly
- 1 (5-ounce) package spring mix salad
- ¼ medium red onion, peeled and diced
- 1 cup cherry tomatoes
- ¼ cup edible mini hibiscus flowers
- 1 cup sliced fresh strawberries

1. To make Creamy Strawberry Dressing: Place all ingredients in a blender and blend 1 minute or until smooth.
2. To Assemble: Place spring mix in a large bowl. Drizzle on desired amount of Creamy Strawberry Dressing and toss to combine (excess can be stored in a sealed plastic container in the refrigerator up to 1 week). Sprinkle on red onion, cherry tomatoes, edible hibiscus flowers, and sliced strawberries. Serve immediately.

Disney Parks Info

This salad is one of the over one hundred fifty Walt Disney World Fiftieth Anniversary special food offerings that the Disney Parks released just for the occasion. Instead of putting them all out at once, they did so in phases over the course of the eighteen-month celebration.

Our Famous Cobb Salad

The Hollywood Brown Derby, Disney's Hollywood Studios

Large enough to be a whole meal for one, or an appetizer for two or three, this yummy and hearty salad is a great energy boost for a day at Disney's Hollywood Studios or a busy day at home! The salad is served with the toppings in neat lines at The Hollywood Brown Derby, and the server will offer to toss the ingredients together for you. Imagine how surprised your family will be when you offer table-side salad-tossing for them!

SERVES 1

For Dressing
- 3 tablespoons red wine vinegar
- 1 tablespoon lemon juice
- 1 teaspoon minced garlic
- 1 teaspoon Worcestershire sauce
- 2 teaspoons Dijon mustard
- ½ teaspoon granulated sugar
- 3 tablespoons water
- 3 tablespoons olive oil
- ⅓ cup corn oil
- ¼ teaspoon salt
- ⅛ teaspoon ground black pepper

For Assembly
- 3 cups chopped romaine lettuce
- ½ cup cubed roasted turkey
- ¼ cup cooked bacon crumbles
- 2 hard-boiled eggs, diced
- 2 tablespoons crumbled blue cheese
- 1 medium avocado, peeled, pitted, and diced
- 1 medium Roma tomato, diced

1. To make Dressing: Add all ingredients to a blender and pulse 1 minute or until combined. If not using immediately, pour Dressing into a pint jar, cover, and store in the refrigerator up to 1 week.
2. To Assemble: Place romaine lettuce on a large plate. Lay each ingredient in a line, one next to another, on top of romaine. Drizzle desired amount of Dressing on salad and toss to combine before serving.

Disney Parks Tip

The Hollywood Brown Derby is near the stunning Mickey & Minnie's Runaway Railway. Opened in 2020, this ride uses incredibly detailed projection technology that brings the Mickey cartoons to life right before your eyes as trackless vehicles travel in unexpected directions. It is a ride you won't want to miss!

Peanut Butter, Chocolate-Hazelnut Spread, and Banana Sandwich

••••• Tortuga Tavern, Magic Kingdom •••••

Tortuga Tavern is a nice little Quick Service restaurant located across from Pirates of the Caribbean in Adventureland. The catch is that it is only open seasonally. Don't risk it not being open: Make this sandwich at home today! The fillings are things you might already have on hand, but cooking and pressing the sandwich in a buttered pan really melds the flavors together. Your family will flock to the kitchen when they smell this cooking and may react like a band of hungry pirates until they get some!

SERVES 1

2 slices white bread
1 tablespoon chocolate-hazelnut spread
1 tablespoon creamy peanut butter
½ medium ripe banana, peeled and sliced thin
1 tablespoon salted butter
½ cup salted potato chips

1. Place a medium skillet over medium heat.
2. Lay out bread slices. Smear chocolate-hazelnut spread on 1 slice and peanut butter on second slice. Lay banana slices on top of chocolate-hazelnut spread and flip peanut butter side onto bananas.
3. Place butter in preheated pan and allow to just melt. Place sandwich into butter and press down onto sandwich with a spatula or bacon press. Cook 1–3 minutes until underside is golden brown, flip, press, and cook an additional 1–3 minutes until bottom is golden brown.
4. Transfer to a cutting board and cut on a diagonal. Serve alongside potato chips.

Lobster Bisque

···· **Coral Reef Restaurant, EPCOT** ····

The only thing better than the view at Coral Reef Restaurant is the seasonal Lobster Bisque! It's creamy and delicious with just the right amount of lobster; people will cross a whole ocean to get their hands on it. If you are dining at Coral Reef Restaurant, request a table by the wall of the restaurant that looks out onto The Seas with Nemo & Friends pavilion, a *5.7-million-gallon* saltwater aquarium. Sharks, sea turtles, fish of all kinds, and even scuba divers can be seen gliding through the water as you slurp your soup.

SERVES 6

For Lobster Stock

- 2 (4-ounce) lobster tails, meat removed, divided
- 4 cups seafood stock
- 2 cups water
- 1 teaspoon dried basil
- 1 teaspoon dried oregano
- 1 teaspoon dried thyme
- 1 teaspoon dried sage
- 1 teaspoon dried lavender
- 1 teaspoon salt

For Bisque

- 2 tablespoons salted butter
- ½ cup diced yellow onion
- ½ cup diced carrots
- ½ cup diced celery
- 2 teaspoons minced garlic

1. To make Lobster Stock: In a large pot over high heat, add lobster tails, seafood stock, water, and seasonings. Bring to a boil, then reduce heat to low and simmer 15 minutes.
2. Add lobster tail meat to pot, cover with lid, and cook 5 minutes or until meat is cooked through and has an internal temperature of 140°F. Remove meat and cut into small pieces. Set aside. Strain stock through a medium-mesh strainer and set aside.
3. To make Bisque: In a clean large pot over medium heat, add butter. Once melted, add onion, carrots, and celery and cook 5–8 minutes until soft. Add garlic and cook 1–2 minutes more until fragrant. Add tomato paste and cook an additional 1–2 minutes until everything is well combined.
4. Add flour to pot and stir well to coat. Cook 2 minutes, stirring frequently. Add in wine and cook 5 minutes to reduce.

- 1 tablespoon tomato paste
- 2 tablespoons all-purpose flour
- ¾ cup dry white wine
- ½ cup heavy whipping cream
- ½ teaspoon salt
- ½ teaspoon ground black pepper

5. Slowly pour prepared Lobster Stock into pot and stir thoroughly. Reduce heat to low and simmer 30 minutes.
6. Blend with an immersion blender or in batches in a blender until entire soup is blended and smooth. Add in lobster chunks and heavy whipping cream and stir to combine. Season with salt and pepper and serve immediately.

Orange Chicken

••••• **Lotus Blossom Café, EPCOT** •••••

Did you know that Orange Chicken originated in North America and not China, as some believe? However, the flavors were inspired by those of the Hunan province of China, and this is why Orange Chicken is such a staple of American Chinese cuisine today. This dish is served as a whole meal combo in the Park and includes a scoop of white rice, a seasonal vegetable, and a crispy egg roll. You can prepare the whole combo, or just the Orange Chicken—whatever works in your meal plan!

SERVES 4

For Fried Chicken

48 ounces vegetable oil, for frying
¼ cup all-purpose flour
1 tablespoon cornstarch
1 teaspoon salt
1 teaspoon ground black pepper
1 teaspoon onion powder
1 teaspoon paprika
½ teaspoon ground ginger
4 (½-pound) boneless, skinless chicken breasts, cut in ½" cubes
3 large eggs, beaten

For Orange Sauce

¾ cup pulp-free orange juice
1½ tablespoons cornstarch
2 tablespoons vegetable oil
3 tablespoons soy sauce
1½ tablespoons mirin
2 tablespoons light brown sugar
2 teaspoons minced ginger
2 teaspoons minced garlic
½ teaspoon ground black pepper

1. To make Fried Chicken: In a large pot over medium heat, preheat oil to 350°F. Line a plate with paper towels.
2. In a large bowl, mix flour, cornstarch, salt, pepper, onion powder, paprika, and ginger, then add chicken cubes and toss to coat.
3. Place beaten eggs in a shallow dish. Dip cubes in eggs, then dip back into flour mixture.
4. Working in batches, cook chicken in preheated oil 2–3 minutes until internal temperature reaches 165°F, then transfer to prepared plate.
5. To make Orange Sauce: In a medium saucepan or wok over medium heat, add all ingredients. Bring to a boil and then reduce heat to low. Add in Fried Chicken and stir gently to coat. Serve.

Margherita Flatbreads

Mama Melrose's Ristorante Italiano, Disney's Hollywood Studios

"Mama" had moved from Sicily, Italy, to Hollywood, California, as a young girl to pursue her dream of acting. Most of the roles she landed were as extras in films, so she had some time to make Italian food for her friends to eat after a day of work on set. The restaurant is filled with mismatched furniture and decor, as she got each piece one by one from movies she was in! This dish is called a flatbread, but it certainly looks and tastes just like a pizza! Be like Mama and make a batch for your friends.

YIELDS 2 (12") FLATBREADS

1 cup warm water (110°F)

1 teaspoon rapid-rise yeast

1 teaspoon plus 1 tablespoon olive oil, divided

2¼ cups all-purpose flour plus extra for dusting

2 cups marinara sauce

2 (16-ounce) packages fresh mozzarella cheese slices

16 fresh basil leaves

1. In a large bowl, mix water, yeast, 1 teaspoon olive oil, and 2¼ cups flour with your hands until just combined and dough is shaggy. Cover with a clean kitchen towel and let rest 15 minutes.
2. Grease two large bowls with oil.
3. After 15 minutes, knead dough by hand 3 minutes or until dough is well combined and soft. Cut into two equal-sized pieces and place each piece in a prepared bowl. Cover with two clean kitchen towels and let rise in a warm place 1 hour.
4. Place a full baking sheet upside down in oven and preheat to 550°F.
5. Turn each dough ball out onto a lightly floured surface. Coat your hands in olive oil and carefully push each ball into a round 12" crust.
6. Spread 1 cup sauce onto each crust, leaving a ½" margin around the edges. Top each with mozzarella slices and basil leaves.
7. Carefully remove baking sheet from oven and place 1 flatbread onto sheet. Return to oven and bake 5–7 minutes until crust is browned and cheese is melted. Repeat with second flatbread. Drizzle each flatbread with ½ tablespoon olive oil, slice, and serve immediately.

"Totchos"

Woody's Lunch Box, Disney's Hollywood Studios

Are they nachos? Are they potato tots? Perhaps the Disney chefs couldn't decide either, so they went with the name "Totchos"—quotation marks and all! This amalgamation of potato tots covered in toppings is a fan favorite at Woody's Lunch Box, and mobile ordering windows tend to fill up quickly for this Quick Service restaurant. But you don't have to move like there is a snake in your boot when you make a batch at home: There's no rush to enjoying "Totchos" in your own kitchen!

SERVES 1

For Beef and Bean Chili
- 1 teaspoon vegetable oil
- ½ medium yellow onion, peeled and diced
- 1 teaspoon minced garlic
- ½ pound lean ground beef
- 2 (15-ounce) cans black beans, including liquid
- 2 teaspoons dried oregano
- 2 teaspoons dried basil
- 1 tablespoon ground cumin
- 2 teaspoons curry powder
- 2 teaspoons salt
- ½ teaspoon ground black pepper
- 2 teaspoons red wine vinegar

For Assembly
- 2 cups frozen potato tots, prepared
- ¼ cup shredded sharp Cheddar cheese
- ¼ cup queso, warmed
- 2 tablespoons diced Roma tomatoes
- ¼ cup corn chips
- 1 tablespoon sour cream
- 1 teaspoon chopped fresh green onion

1. To make Beef and Bean Chili: In a large pot over medium heat, add oil, onion, and garlic. Cook until onion is translucent, about 3 minutes. Add ground beef and stir until browned, about 6 minutes. Add remaining ingredients, stir, then reduce heat to low and simmer uncovered 1 hour.
2. To Assemble: Place tots into a bowl. Add desired amount of Beef and Bean Chili (leftovers can be kept in an airtight container in the refrigerator for up to 1 week). Sprinkle with cheese and drizzle with queso, then add tomatoes, corn chips, and a scoop of sour cream. Top with green onion. Serve immediately.

Shrimp Salad Roll

········ **Dockside Diner, Disney's Hollywood Studios** ········

If you're looking for a salad roll that's "shrimply" irresistible, look no further! Sold at a quaint boat in Echo Lake of Disney's Hollywood Studios, nothing speaks summer like a yummy Shrimp Salad Roll. Tossed in rémoulade sauce and stuffed into a buttery bun, this dish is served with chips; you don't need more on the side than that—that would be "over-krill"!

SERVES 1

For Pickled Fennel
- 1 large bulb fennel, fronds removed
- 1 cup apple cider vinegar
- 1 cup water
- 2 teaspoons granulated sugar
- 1 teaspoon salt
- ½ teaspoon fennel seeds
- ½ teaspoon yellow mustard seeds
- 1 teaspoon black peppercorns

For Rémoulade Sauce
- ¼ cup mayonnaise
- ½ teaspoon yellow mustard
- ½ teaspoon Creole seasoning
- ½ teaspoon prepared horseradish
- 1 teaspoon dill pickle juice

1. To make Pickled Fennel: Slice fennel bulb thinly and put slices into a pint-sized Mason jar.
2. In a small saucepan over medium heat, add remaining ingredients. Bring to a boil, then pour over fennel slices in Mason jar, making sure fennel is completely covered. Let cool at room temperature, about 45 minutes, then cover and refrigerate overnight.
3. To make Rémoulade Sauce: Mix all ingredients in a small bowl. Cover and refrigerate 2 hours.
4. To Assemble: Heat a small skillet over medium heat. Grease with nonstick cooking spray and add shrimp. Cook 2–3 minutes per side until cooked through and brown on both sides. Remove pan from heat.

For Assembly

6 jumbo raw shrimp, tails off and deveined

½ cup fresh arugula

1 small Roma tomato, diced

1 medium radish, sliced thin

1 long brioche butter bun, sliced open

5. Place several strands of Pickled Fennel into a medium bowl (leftovers can be kept sealed in Mason jar for up to 2 weeks) and add in shrimp, arugula, tomato, and radish. Drizzle with desired amount of Rémoulade Sauce (excess can be sealed and refrigerated up to 1 week) and toss to coat. Scoop into brioche bun and serve immediately.

Cooking Hack

If you can't get fresh shrimp from your local fishmonger, just use frozen shrimp from the freezer section of your grocery store! Let it thaw according to the package instructions and cook following this recipe's instructions.

Lettuce Cups

Yak & Yeti Restaurant, Disney's Animal Kingdom

Step out of the sun and have a bite of this crisp, refreshing, yummy lunch. Yak & Yeti Restaurant melds flavors from across Southeast Asia and beyond. Unlike most other restaurants at Disney, Yak & Yeti Restaurant is owned and operated by Landry's Inc. and not The Walt Disney Company. This means that approval of dishes goes through completely different pipelines, and in-house chefs has more control over what appears on the menu. Their vision and creativity provide the incredible dishes offered each day!

SERVES 4

- 1 tablespoon plus 1 teaspoon sesame oil, divided
- ½ medium yellow onion, peeled and diced
- 3 teaspoons minced garlic
- 1 pound ground chicken breast
- ½ cup hoisin sauce, divided
- 1 tablespoon oyster sauce
- 1 teaspoon grated ginger
- ¼ cup water chestnuts, diced
- 2 stalks green onion, diced, whites discarded
- ¼ cup shredded carrots
- ¼ cup peeled and shredded cucumber
- ½ medium head iceberg lettuce

1. Heat 1 tablespoon sesame oil in a large nonstick pan or wok over medium heat. Add onion and cook until soft and translucent, about 5 minutes. Add garlic and cook 2 minutes more. Add ground chicken and cook until browned and cooked through and has an internal temperature of 165°F, 5–8 minutes.

2. Add ¼ cup hoisin sauce, oyster sauce, 1 teaspoon sesame oil, and grated ginger to pan or wok. Stir to combine. Add water chestnuts and green onion and stir and cook 3 minutes more, then remove from heat. Scoop mixture into a serving bowl. Garnish with carrots and cucumber.

3. Separate leaves of lettuce to make cups and serve alongside chicken filling and remaining ¼ cup hoisin sauce for dipping. To eat, scoop desired amount of chicken filling into one lettuce cup and drizzle with sauce.

Poblano Mac & Cheese

Paradise Garden Grill, Disney California Adventure

If you're afraid of the heat of a poblano pepper, don't be! Once it has been roasted and the skin and seeds have been removed, all that is left is a lovely flavor with very little spice that complements this creamy macaroni and cheese perfectly. Paradise Garden Grill is by Goofy's Sky School at Disney California Adventure and sometimes holds performances from local bands. Be sure to swing by to see who's playing next time you're there.

SERVES 8

- 1 large poblano pepper
- ¼ cup salted butter
- 1½ cups heavy whipping cream
- ½ cup whole milk
- ½ teaspoon garlic salt
- 1 cup shredded Gruyère cheese
- 1 cup shredded mozzarella cheese, divided
- ½ cup shredded sharp Cheddar cheese
- 1 pound dry extra-large macaroni, cooked according to package directions
- 2 cups crushed cornflakes

1. Preheat oven to 425°F.
2. Place poblano pepper in a small, ungreased oven-safe dish and bake 15 minutes, flipping halfway through bake time.
3. Remove from oven and cover with dish lid or foil and allow to sit 15 minutes. Remove poblano from dish and remove skin and seeds and then dice. Set aside.
4. Reduce oven temperature to 400°F. Grease a 9" × 13" baking dish with nonstick cooking spray and set aside.
5. In a large saucepan over medium heat, melt butter. Add in cream, milk, and garlic salt. Slowly add in cheeses, reserving ½ cup mozzarella. Stir until cheeses melt and sauce is creamy, about 2 minutes.
6. Add in cooked macaroni and diced poblano and stir to coat. Pour mixture into prepared dish and sprinkle with cornflakes and reserved mozzarella. Bake 15–20 minutes until cheese is bubbling. Remove from oven and allow to cool 10 minutes before serving.

Smokehouse Chicken Salad

Flame Tree Barbecue, Disney's Animal Kingdom

This salad stands out from others in a lot of ways, but one of its most unique elements is the croutons made from corn bread. Delicious little corn-flavored cubes deliver an added crunch. Flame Tree Barbecue at Disney's Animal Kingdom has lots of outdoor seating, so you may want to consider it if you're looking for a place to sit down and eat on a busy Park day. You may even catch some characters walking by, like Kevin from the movie *Up*! She walks around Discovery Island and interacts with all the guests.

SERVES 1

For Croutons
- 1 cup 1" prepared corn bread cubes
- 1 tablespoon olive oil
- ½ teaspoon salt

For Salad
- 3 cups mixed greens
- ½ cup shredded rotisserie chicken
- ¼ cup shredded smoked Cheddar cheese
- ¼ cup diced Granny Smith apple
- 2 tablespoons dried cranberries
- 2 tablespoons crispy fried onions
- 2 tablespoons ranch dressing
- 1 tablespoon barbecue sauce

1. To make Croutons: Preheat oven to 350°F. Line a half baking sheet with parchment paper.
2. Spread out corn bread cubes on sheet. Drizzle with olive oil and bake 10–15 minutes until cubes are golden brown. Sprinkle with salt and allow to cool to room temperature, about 45 minutes.
3. To make Salad: Place mixed greens on a large plate and cover with chicken, Cheddar cheese, apple, cranberries, crispy fried onions, and Croutons. Combine ranch dressing and barbecue sauce in a small bowl and drizzle desired amount on top. Serve immediately.

Not So Little Chicken Sandwich

Pym Test Kitchen, Disney California Adventure

This sandwich packs a supersized punch of deliciousness. Get ready to be transported into a quantum realm of flavors. It features a huge chicken patty between two itty-bitty bun layers, as well as a generous drizzling of sauce over the chicken. Feel free to adjust the amount you drizzle based on personal preference. To round out the meal, serve with potato tots.

SERVES 1

For Pickled Cabbage Slaw

- 1 cup shredded red cabbage
- ½ cup apple cider vinegar
- ½ cup water
- 1 tablespoon granulated sugar
- 1 teaspoon minced garlic
- 1 teaspoon salt
- ½ teaspoon ground black pepper

For Fried Chicken Patty

- 48 ounces vegetable oil, for frying
- ½ cup flour
- 1 large egg, beaten
- 1 cup plain bread crumbs
- 1 (½-pound) boneless, skinless chicken breast
- 1 teaspoon salt

1. To make Pickled Cabbage Slaw: Place cabbage in a pint-sized Mason jar. Add in remaining ingredients, cover, and let sit at room temperature for 30 minutes.
2. To make Fried Chicken Patty: Pour oil into a large pot over medium heat and bring to 350°F. Line a plate with paper towels.
3. Place flour, beaten egg, and bread crumbs in three shallow bowls.
4. Pound chicken with a meat tenderizer until about ⅓" flat. Dab dry with a paper towel and season with salt on both sides. Dredge chicken in flour, then egg, then bread crumbs. Carefully lower breaded patty into hot oil and fry 2–3 minutes per side until internal temperature reaches 165°F. Transfer from oil to prepared plate and allow to cool 10 minutes.

(continued)

For Assembly

1 brioche slider bun

1 tablespoon teriyaki sauce

1 tablespoon sriracha mayo

1 tablespoon diced green onion

5. **To Assemble:** Layer slider bun bottom with Fried Chicken Patty, drizzle with teriyaki and sriracha mayo, top with desired amount of Pickled Cabbage Slaw (excess can be stored in a sealed container in the refrigerator up to 3 days), sprinkle with green onion, and finish with bun top. Serve.

Disney Parks Tip

Avengers Campus is at Disney California Adventure and is the place to see and hang out with all your favorite Marvel superheroes. At certain times of day, Spider-Man can be seen swinging through the air, or the Dora Milaje teaching guests how to fight like a true Wakandan.

······ **CHAPTER 5** ······

Appetizers and Snacks

Now that you've eaten up breakfast and lunch in the previous chapters, let's dive into the appetizers and snacks that will leave you satisfied until the main event of dinner. Whether you're looking for a start to your fancy à la carte or prix fixe meal, or needing a snack on the go, this chapter will grant your dining wishes.

With such offerings as crisp salads, loaded nachos, fried cheeses, and even a bread you can eat with a spoon, you're sure to discover something new in addition to your go-to Disney Parks favorites. A great benefit of creating these small bites at home is getting to eat them whenever you want, including as an entire entrée if you'd like! Enjoy a batch to yourself or make up a full meal with a bunch of different recipes from this chapter.

Fried Pickles

Carnation Café, Disneyland

Disneyland has always served large dill pickles at carts and stands across the Park. Guests buy these massive snacks and carry them around, taking the occasional bite. They have become an iconic theme park treat! Carnation Café wanted to bring the popular pickle product to its restaurant, but level it up a bit. These Fried Pickles are delicious and crispy and are great vehicles for a tasty sauce. Fry them up fresh for your friends right before serving to keep them extra crispy!

YIELDS 6 PICKLES

- 48 ounces vegetable oil, for frying
- ½ cup all-purpose flour
- 1 large egg
- 1 cup panko bread crumbs
- ¼ cup mayonnaise
- 2 tablespoons ranch dressing
- 1½ teaspoons sriracha sauce
- ¼ teaspoon salt
- ¼ teaspoon ground black pepper
- 1½ teaspoons lime juice
- 6 dill pickle spears
- 1 teaspoon chopped fresh parsley leaves

1. Pour vegetable oil into a medium saucepan over medium heat and heat to 375°F. Line a plate with paper towels.
2. Place flour in a shallow dish, place egg in a separate shallow dish and whisk, and pour bread crumbs into a third shallow dish.
3. In a small bowl, stir together mayonnaise, ranch dressing, sriracha, salt, pepper, and lime juice.
4. Once oil is up to temperature, pat 1 pickle spear dry with a paper towel, then dredge in flour, dip in egg, and cover with panko. Carefully lower spear into hot oil and fry 2–3 minutes until breading is golden brown. Transfer to prepared plate. Repeat with remaining spears, being sure to fry only 3 at a time to avoid crowding the pan. Let cool 5 minutes. Pour prepared dipping sauce into a small bowl and sprinkle with parsley. Serve.

Five-Blossom Bread

Oga's Cantina at Disneyland and Disney's Hollywood Studios

This dish originated on the lush planet of Naboo, and rumors also say that it was a favorite snack of Queen Amidala. It's easy to see why! Each bite of the fluffy pretzel knots dipped in both puffy mustard sauce and golden cheese is fit for royalty. If you want to share this with a crowd, simply make the pretzels into bites or smaller knots so everyone can have some.

SERVES 2

For Pretzel Knots

2½ cups warm water (110°F), divided
1½ tablespoons dark molasses
1 (0.25-ounce) package active dry yeast
3 tablespoons salted butter, softened
4 cups all-purpose flour
½ teaspoon salt
2 tablespoons baking soda
2 tablespoons Hawaiian black sea salt
2 tablespoons salted butter, melted

1. To make Pretzel Knots: Combine 1½ cups warm water, molasses, and yeast in a small bowl and let bloom 10 minutes or until froth forms on top.
2. In the bowl of a stand mixer fitted with dough hook, cream softened butter, flour, and salt. Add yeast mixture and knead with dough hook on low speed 8 minutes or until dough is soft and elastic.
3. Cut dough into four equal pieces and work with one piece at a time. Slowly and carefully roll and pull dough into a 2' rope. Tie the rope into a knot and tuck the ends back into the center of the knot. Repeat with remaining dough pieces. Set aside and allow to rest 20 minutes.
4. Place a full-sized baking sheet in the oven and preheat to 500°F.
5. Pour remaining 1 cup water and baking soda in a small saucepan over medium-high heat and bring to a boil. Remove from heat and brush generously onto each pretzel knot and sprinkle each with Hawaiian black sea salt.
6. Carefully slide pretzels onto heated baking sheet in oven with two spatulas and bake 8–12 minutes until deep brown. Remove from oven and brush with melted butter.

(continued) ▶

For Honey-Mustard Cream Foam

- ½ cup mayonnaise
- 2 tablespoons yellow mustard
- ¼ teaspoon onion powder
- ¼ teaspoon garlic powder
- 2 tablespoons honey
- ½ cup heavy whipping cream
- 4 teaspoons microgreens

For Calabrian Cheese Sauce

- 2 tablespoons salted butter
- 2 tablespoons all-purpose flour
- 1 cup whole milk
- 8 ounces shredded sharp Cheddar cheese
- 3 tablespoons pickled jalapeño juice
- 1 teaspoon sriracha

7. To make Honey-Mustard Cream Foam: Whisk all ingredients except microgreens together in a medium bowl and carefully pour into an aluminum cream maker. Add charging cannister and shake gently.
8. Completely invert and spray foam into two dipping cups. Sprinkle each with microgreens and set aside. (If you don't have an aluminum cream maker, simply pour mix into a stand mixer fitted with whisk attachment and whip until soft peaks form.)
9. To make Calabrian Cheese Sauce: In a small saucepan over medium heat, add butter. Once melted, stir in flour and cook 2–3 minutes. Stir in milk and simmer 1–3 minutes until bubbles form around the edges.
10. Reduce heat to low and sprinkle in cheese while continuing to stir. Once cheese is melted, add in pickled jalapeño juice and sriracha. Remove from heat and pour into two dipping cups and set aside.
11. To serve, divide Pretzel Knots on two plates and serve each plate with 1 cup of Honey-Mustard Cream Foam and 1 cup of Calabrian Cheese Sauce for dipping.

Disney Parks Tip

Oga's Cantina is a Star Wars–themed bar in Galaxy's Edge located at Disneyland in California and Disney's Hollywood Studios in Florida. However, while most of the drinks are the same at both locations, these pretzels can be found only at the Oga's in California. Who knows, maybe one day they will migrate over!

Pomme Frites

Cafe Orleans, Disneyland

Pomme Frites simply means "potato fries" in French. These potato fries are adorned with Parmesan cheese, herbs, and spices to make them extra delicious. Next time you're having a large group over to watch a football game (or maybe the Tour de France), make a large pan of these for everyone to munch on. You can even make half the pan with Parmesan and half without or add cayenne to some of the fries for those looking for a spicier bite.

SERVES 2

- 2 cups frozen skinny French fries
- 1 tablespoon grated Parmesan cheese
- 1 teaspoon garlic powder
- ½ teaspoon kosher salt
- 1 tablespoon chopped fresh parsley
- ¼ cup Thousand Island dressing
- 2 tablespoons mayonnaise
- ½ teaspoon minced garlic
- ¼ teaspoon Dijon mustard
- ¼ teaspoon Cajun seasoning

1. Prepare fries according to package instructions. In a small bowl, mix Parmesan cheese, garlic powder, and salt and sprinkle on fries while still hot. Pour onto a serving plate and sprinkle with parsley.
2. Combine Thousand Island dressing, mayonnaise, minced garlic, Dijon mustard, and Cajun seasoning in a small bowl. Serve alongside fries.

Serving Suggestion

At Cafe Orleans, these are often served alongside Battered & Fried Monte Cristo sandwiches (see recipe in Chapter 6). Plan to make both together for the authentic experience!

Country Seasonal Salad

····· **Be Our Guest Restaurant, Magic Kingdom** ·····

This salad has a je ne sais quoi. And if you don't know what that means, give it a taste and find out! Fresh peaches lend a spring-y flavor. If you're looking for something light and fun to complement your next showstopping meal, this is it. So, be *my* guest and make this recipe!

SERVES 1

For Seasonal Vinaigrette Dressing
1 large fresh peach, peeled, pitted, and sliced
3 tablespoons olive oil
1 tablespoon apple cider vinegar
1 teaspoon salt

For Salad
2 cups spring mix salad
¼ cup mixed fresh raspberries and blackberries
2 tablespoons candied walnuts

1. To make Seasonal Vinaigrette Dressing: Add all ingredients to a blender and blend until well combined, about 1 minute. Pour into a sealable container and refrigerate 1 hour.
2. To make Salad: Place spring mix on a large plate. Drizzle with desired amount of Seasonal Vinaigrette Dressing (leftovers can be refrigerated up to 1 week). Sprinkle on berries and walnuts and serve immediately.

House-Made Peach Applesauce

••••• **Be Our Guest Restaurant, Magic Kingdom** •••••

Yummy apples and peaches meld together in a creamy bite; you'll be glad you have a whole pot of this dish! Be Our Guest Restaurant is inside of Beast's Castle, and the Beast himself occasionally roams the dining rooms to thank all the guests for coming to his home.

SERVES 8

- 3 pounds Gala apples, peeled, cored, and sliced
- 2 cups frozen peach slices
- 1/4 cup honey
- 3/4 cup granulated sugar
- 1/2 cup water

1. Add all ingredients to an electric pressure cooker. Cover and seal lid, then set to high pressure cook 5 minutes. Once cooking is complete, allow pressure to release naturally, about 15 minutes.
2. Using an immersion blender, or carefully pouring into a blender in batches, pulse several times to achieve desired consistency. Cover and refrigerate until completely cool, about 2 hours. Scoop into bowls and serve.

Cooking Hack

When you're blending, make it to your desired consistency. Smooth or chunky, the choice is yours! Don't worry—Belle, Beast, Lumière, and Cogsworth will approve.

Carpaccio di Manzo

Tutto Italia Ristorante, EPCOT

Truly stepping out from your stereotypical "theme park" fare, Wagyu beef is firmly in the category of luxury. You may even feel like you've switched EPCOT pavilions since Wagyu beef is from Japanese cows. The Italians must agree that this is the best beef on Earth, as they serve it at their pavilion in this gorgeous dish. Although the beef is incredibly tender, the real star is the lemon dressing, which adds a pop of flavor that you'll be wanting to put on everything you make.

SERVES 1

1 teaspoon lemon juice
1 teaspoon granulated sugar
½ teaspoon minced garlic
½ teaspoon salt
¼ cup mayonnaise
1 cup arugula
8 thin (about 3" round) slices Wagyu beef
2 thin (2" × 3") slices Parmesan cheese
½ teaspoon fresh cracked black pepper

1. In a small bowl, combine lemon juice, sugar, garlic, salt, and mayonnaise. Decant into a squirt bottle and set aside.
2. Toss arugula with 1 tablespoon lemon dressing in a small bowl.
3. Lay Wagyu slices in a circle on a large dinner plate. Pile arugula salad in center of circle and top with Parmesan slices. Squirt dressing around Wagyu slices (leftover dressing can be refrigerated in bottle up to 1 week) and crack black pepper over dish. Serve immediately.

Chicken Pot Stickers

Lotus Blossom Café, EPCOT

Many months of the year, EPCOT festival booths offering delicious small bites from a variety of countries line the walkways. However, these Chicken Pot Stickers can be found year-round at Lotus Blossom Café, just off the main path into the China pavilion. You may need to order a few since only three come in each serving. When you make this at home, though, you'll be prepared to serve the whole family—and more! Just 1 pound of chicken makes eight servings.

SERVES 8

- 3 cups angel hair coleslaw
- 1 teaspoon salt
- 1 large egg
- ¼ cup diced green onions
- 2 tablespoons soy sauce
- 2 teaspoons minced garlic
- ½ teaspoon ground black pepper
- 1 pound ground chicken breast
- ½ cup vegetable oil, divided
- 1 (12-ounce) package circular pot sticker wrappers (about 50 wrappers)
- ¼ cup water
- 1 cup soy sauce

1. Place coleslaw in a strainer in the sink and sprinkle with salt. Allow salt to remove water from coleslaw, about 10 minutes.
2. In a large bowl, add egg, green onions, soy sauce, garlic, and pepper and beat to combine. Squeeze coleslaw against edges of strainer to remove as much liquid as possible, then add coleslaw to egg mixture and stir to combine. Add in chicken and use your hands to mix well.
3. Place a large nonstick pan over medium heat and add 2 tablespoons vegetable oil. Fill pot sticker wrappers with about 1 tablespoon filling each. Wet your finger with water and run along circular edges of wrappers. Fold each wrapper in half over filling and crimp with fingers to form a tight seal.
4. Working in batches, place 10–12 pot stickers into pan (crimp side up). Allow to cook 2–3 minutes until bottoms are browned.
5. Pour water into pan and cover with lid. Cook 3–4 minutes more. Remove lid, lay pot stickers onto one side, cover, and cook an additional 3–4 minutes until internal temperature reaches 160°F. Remove from heat and repeat cooking steps with remaining potstickers. Serve with soy sauce on the side for dipping.

Fried Mozzarella

Tony's Town Square Restaurant, Magic Kingdom

Tony's Town Square Restaurant at Magic Kingdom is designed to be the same restaurant where Lady and the Tramp share a plate of spaghetti and meatballs in their original animated film. The cheese from this dish is so stretchy, you can almost reenact that scene with cheese instead of pasta! From the patio or atrium of Tony's, you can peek at the Disney Festival of Fantasy Parade as it comes down Main Street, U.S.A. If you're enjoying this appetizer or snack at home, cue up the parade on *YouTube* and enjoy it at your kitchen table.

SERVES 2

- 48 ounces vegetable oil, for frying
- 2 cups Italian bread crumbs
- 2 large eggs, beaten
- 1 (8-ounce) block mozzarella cheese, sliced lengthwise into 8 strips
- 2 tablespoons fresh parsley
- ½ cup marinara sauce

1. Pour oil into a large pot over medium heat and preheat temperature to 350°F. Line a large plate with paper towels.
2. Place bread crumbs and beaten eggs in two shallow dishes each.
3. Dip cheese strips one at a time in bread crumbs, eggs, then bread crumbs again, making sure to completely coat cheese in crumbs.
4. Carefully lower each coated cheese strip one at a time into hot oil. Fry 2–3 strips at a time 2 minutes, flip, then fry 2 minutes more. Transfer to prepared plate.
5. Divide cheese between two plates. Sprinkle each plate with 1 tablespoon parsley and serve with ¼ cup marinara sauce each for dipping.

Baby Iceberg Wedge Salad

······· **Le Cellier Steakhouse, EPCOT** ·······

A wedge salad is a salad that isn't tossed but is instead assembled with the whole head of lettuce cut into chunks that the diner dives into with a fork and knife. This unique serving method gives the dish a crunch that tossed salads can't rival. Le Cellier Steakhouse is tucked within the Canada pavilion at EPCOT and often has a sold-out reservation list due to its popularity over yummy dishes like this one. Skip the reservation and enjoy a Baby Iceberg Wedge Salad at home.

SERVES 1

For Buttermilk Ranch
- ¼ cup sour cream
- ¼ cup buttermilk
- 2 tablespoons mayonnaise
- 1½ teaspoons minced garlic
- ½ teaspoon salt
- ¼ teaspoon ground black pepper
- ½ teaspoon dried dill
- 2 tablespoons finely chopped fresh chives
- 1 teaspoon lemon juice

For Marinated Tomatoes
- ½ medium shallot, peeled and minced
- 1 tablespoon lime juice
- 1 teaspoon minced garlic
- 2 teaspoons minced fresh basil
- 1 tablespoon balsamic vinegar
- ¼ cup olive oil
- 1 cup Toy Box or cherry tomatoes, halved

For Assembly
- ½ medium head baby iceberg lettuce, quartered
- 1 tablespoon cooked and shelled edamame
- 1 tablespoon crumbled applewood-smoked bacon
- 1 tablespoon crumbled blue cheese
- 1 tablespoon crispy fried onions

1. To make Buttermilk Ranch: Combine all ingredients in a medium bowl. Refrigerate 30 minutes.
2. To make Marinated Tomatoes: Combine all ingredients in a medium bowl. Refrigerate 30 minutes.
3. To Assemble: Place baby iceberg lettuce quarters on a large plate. Drizzle with desired amount of Buttermilk Ranch (refrigerate any leftovers up to 3 days) and sprinkle with edamame, bacon, blue cheese, and fried onions. Place Marinated Tomatoes on top and discard excess marinade. Serve immediately.

Spoon Bread

••••• **The Hollywood Brown Derby, Disney's Hollywood Studios** •••••

Spoon Bread is almost like corn bread but softer and designed to be eaten with a spoon right out of the baking dish. That way you don't need to hold back in slathering plenty of butter on top! The Hollywood Brown Derby changes its flavored butter seasonally, but the Lavender-Honey Butter really stands out. Providing sweetness and floral tones, this flavor shines against the corn backdrop of the Spoon Bread.

SERVES 10

For Lavender-Honey Butter

- ½ cup salted butter, softened
- ½ teaspoon dried lavender flowers, crushed fine
- 3 teaspoons honey

For Spoon Bread

- 1 (8.5-ounce) box "Jiffy" Corn Muffin Mix
- 1 (14.75-ounce) can cream-style corn
- 1 cup canned whole-kernel corn, drained
- ¾ cup sour cream
- ¼ cup whole-milk plain yogurt
- ¼ cup salted butter, melted
- 2 large eggs
- 3 tablespoons granulated sugar
- ½ teaspoon salt

1. To make Lavender-Honey Butter: Mix ingredients together in a small bowl and place in refrigerator to set while making Spoon Bread.
2. To make Spoon Bread: Preheat oven to 375°F. Place ten small ramekins on a baking sheet and grease each with nonstick cooking spray.
3. Add all ingredients to a blender. Blend 1–2 minutes, scraping down sides, to combine all ingredients and break down corn pieces.
4. Pour mixture into ramekins to fill each ½ full. Bake 20–30 minutes until a knife inserted in the center comes out clean.
5. To serve, add a generous scoop of Lavender-Honey Butter to each ramekin of Spoon Bread while still hot and serve immediately.

Mix It Up!

If lavender isn't your jam, feel free to leave it out! Either omit it entirely, or swap in a flavor you do like. Some suggestions: cinnamon, rosemary, or oregano!

Parmesan Chips

Fairfax Fare, Disney's Hollywood Studios

Located across from The Twilight Zone Tower of Terror attraction, Fairfax Fare serves up snacks and treats to munch on while you consider riding the attraction or not. Tower of Terror plunges riders thirteen floors (or 130 feet) in an elevator at speeds up to 39 miles per hour. At home, you can enjoy these chips fright-free! Using popcorn seasoning evenly coats the chips in a fine powder of flavor just like how they are served at Disney's Hollywood Studios.

SERVES 1

48 ounces vegetable oil, for frying

1 russet potato, peeled and sliced thin lengthwise

½ teaspoon garlic Parmesan popcorn seasoning

½ teaspoon sour cream and onion popcorn seasoning

1. Pour oil into a deep fryer or large pot over medium heat and preheat to 350°F. Line a plate with paper towels.
2. Place potato slices in a medium bowl and rinse several times with cold water to remove extra starch. Dab dry with a paper towel.
3. Once oil is at temperature, carefully place potato slices into hot oil and allow to fry 5–7 minutes while stirring frequently until golden brown. Transfer slices with a slotted spoon to a prepared plate.
4. While still hot, transfer chips to a large bowl, sprinkle with seasonings, and toss to coat. Serve immediately.

Fried Herb and Garlic Cheese

······ 50's Prime Time Café, Disney's Hollywood Studios ······

50's Prime Time Café is best known for its nostalgic food options and strict waitstaff. Not stuffy, not arrogant, *strict*. In fact, the waiters and waitresses become your aunts and uncles for the evening and are sure to crack down on you if you don't finish your vegetables. Luckily, you'll need no prodding to finish this gorgeous fruit and cheese plate with a twist—the cheese is fried! Every bite is creamy *and* crispy.

SERVES 4

For Raspberry Sauce
- 2 cups frozen raspberries
- 1 cup granulated sugar
- 1 tablespoon lemon juice

For Bread
- 4 (¼") slices of a sourdough round
- 4 tablespoons olive oil, divided
- 1 teaspoon salt
- ½ teaspoon ground black pepper

For Fried Herb and Garlic Cheese
- 1 (6-ounce) container spreadable creamy garlic and herb cheese wedges
- 48 ounces vegetable oil, for frying

1. To make Raspberry Sauce: In a small saucepan over medium heat, add raspberries, sugar, and lemon juice and stir to combine. Continue to stir and mash berries with a potato masher until mixture comes to a boil, about 5 minutes.
2. Remove from heat and strain though a medium-mesh sieve into a small bowl, discarding solids. Refrigerate 30 minutes.
3. To make Bread: Preheat oven to broil on high. On a baking sheet, lay out sourdough slices. Drizzle with 2 tablespoons olive oil, flip, and drizzle reverse side with remaining 2 tablespoons oil. Sprinkle with salt and pepper and bake 1–3 minutes until golden and crispy.
4. To make Fried Herb and Garlic Cheese: Unwrap cheese wedges and mash 2 wedges together, forming them into a round shape (¼" thick and 3" in diameter). Use plastic wrap to help mash and form the round. Repeat with remaining wedges to make four rounds. Place in freezer, in plastic wrap, 10 minutes.

(continued) ▶

2 cups Italian bread crumbs

2 large eggs

For Assembly

1 tablespoon fresh minced parsley

4 small bunches red grapes

1 large Granny Smith apple, cored and sliced

5. Pour oil into a medium saucepan over medium heat and preheat to 350°F. Line a plate with paper towels.
6. Remove cheese from plastic wrap. Pour bread crumbs in one large bowl and beat eggs in a second large bowl. Dip cheese rounds one at a time in bread crumbs, eggs, then bread crumbs again (making sure cheese is completely covered in bread crumbs).
7. Once oil is at 350°F, carefully lower cheese rounds one at a time into hot oil, frying only two at a time. Fry 1 minute per side and transfer to prepared plate.
8. To Assemble: On each of four small plates, pour about 2–3 tablespoons Raspberry Sauce on one side of plate. Lay Fried Herb and Garlic Cheese on top of Raspberry Sauce and sprinkle with fresh parsley. Place a small bunch of grapes and a couple slices of apple to the side and lay Bread on top of fruit. Enjoy immediately.

Candied Bacon

Pym Test Kitchen, Disney California Adventure

We already know Hank Pym likes to pack a big punch in a tiny package (Ant-Man, anyone?), and this bacon is no exception. Why eat plain ol' bacon when you can make it candy? This is served as a side at Pym Test Kitchen in a small metal bowl reminiscent of something you might use to mix concoctions in a lab. Not that this is unusual for Pym's: Some other items come in a petri dish, a pipette dropper, or a beaker!

SERVES 4

8 slices bacon
¼ cup light brown sugar

1. Preheat oven to 325°F. Line a large baking sheet with aluminum foil.
2. Lay bacon slices on foil-lined sheet and sprinkle each with brown sugar. Lay a sheet of foil on top of bacon and place a second large baking sheet on top of foil.
3. Bake 20 minutes or until bacon is cooked through. Remove from oven and remove top baking sheet. Allow to cool 5 minutes, then serve.

Serving Suggestion

When making the Ever-Expanding Cinna-Pym Toast from Chapter 3, try pairing this bacon instead of plain bacon strips. It works perfectly with the sweetness of the toast.

Ahi Tuna Nachos

Yak & Yeti Restaurant, Disney's Animal Kingdom

Shortly after you enter the Asia section of Disney's Animal Kingdom, you will come upon two dining establishments—and they both have the same name! Yak & Yeti Restaurant and Yak & Yeti Local Food Cafes. The first is a Table Service restaurant dishing up pan-Asian cuisine in a gorgeous Nepalese-decorated dining room. The latter is a Quick Service restaurant that offers Asian eats for those not wanting to dedicate as much time to a meal. These nachos are from the Table Service restaurant and come piled high with irresistible flavors.

SERVES 2

For Asian Slaw
- 1 cup tricolor coleslaw
- ½ cup shredded carrots
- ½ cup chopped fresh cilantro
- 1 tablespoon olive oil
- 1 teaspoon sesame oil
- 2 teaspoons rice wine vinegar
- 1 tablespoon honey
- 1 teaspoon soy sauce
- ½ teaspoon minced garlic
- ½ teaspoon minced ginger
- ⅛ teaspoon salt
- ⅛ teaspoon chili flakes

For Wasabi Aioli
- ¼ cup mayonnaise
- 1 teaspoon prepared wasabi
- 1 teaspoon soy sauce

1. To make Asian Slaw: Stir coleslaw, carrots, and cilantro in a medium bowl. Whisk together remaining ingredients in a small bowl and drizzle desired amount onto vegetables. Leftovers can be refrigerated in a sealed container up to 3 days. Toss to coat.
2. To make Wasabi Aioli: Combine all ingredients in a small bowl.
3. To make Sweet Soy Glaze: Combine all ingredients in a small saucepan over medium-high heat. Bring to a boil, stirring often. Reduce heat to low and simmer 10 minutes. Remove from heat and allow to cool 10 minutes.

For Sweet Soy Glaze

2 teaspoons sesame oil

2 tablespoons minced garlic

2 teaspoons minced ginger

¼ cup soy sauce

3 tablespoons honey

3 tablespoons light brown sugar

1 tablespoon oyster sauce

1 tablespoon apple cider vinegar

For Assembly

2 cups crispy fried wontons

¼ cup chopped sushi-grade ahi tuna

1 tablespoon black sesame seeds

4. To Assemble: Place crispy fried wontons on a large plate. Pile on Asian Slaw and ahi tuna, then drizzle with desired amounts of Wasabi Aioli and Sweet Soy Glaze. (Leftovers can be refrigerated in a sealed container up to 1 week.) Sprinkle with black sesame seeds and serve immediately.

Disney Parks Tip

While you're waiting in line to ride Expedition Everest: Legend of the Forbidden Mountain, you'll notice bells hanging all over the ceilings. These aren't just for decoration; they are meant as a good luck ritual before embarking on your journey up into the mountain. Go ahead and hit them with your hand.

Frijoles Charros

Cocina Cucamonga Mexican Grill, Disney California Adventure

A tasty little side you can pair with any main dish, these Frijoles Charros can be made easily at home: Just pop them in the pressure cooker and you'll be treated to creamy and flavorful beans. Store leftovers in a sealed container in the refrigerator up to one week. Top with shredded cheese and pop in the microwave for 30 seconds to melt for a protein-packed lunch any day of the week.

SERVES 10

- 1 tablespoon olive oil
- 4 teaspoons minced garlic
- 1 cup diced yellow onion
- 2 Roma tomatoes, diced
- 2 tablespoons tomato paste
- ¼ pound bacon strips, diced
- ¼ pound chorizo sausage, crumbled
- 1 tablespoon salt
- 1 tablespoon dried oregano
- 1 tablespoon ground cumin
- 1 tablespoon paprika
- 2 teaspoons ground black pepper
- 2 cups dried pinto beans, rinsed
- 32 ounces vegetable broth
- ½ cup diced red onion
- ¼ cup chopped fresh cilantro

1. Set electric pressure cooker to Sauté and add oil. Add garlic, onion, tomatoes, tomato paste, bacon, and chorizo. Cook 5 minutes or until tender. Add in salt and spices and stir to combine. Add in beans and broth, change pressure cooker to Manual, seal lid, and cook on high 45 minutes.
2. Once complete, allow electric pressure cooker to naturally release pressure 15 minutes, then manually release any pressure remaining. Use a potato masher to mash beans.
3. Scoop into individual bowls and top each with red onion and cilantro. Serve.

Tiffins Signature Bread Service

····· **Tiffins Restaurant, Disney's Animal Kingdom** ·····

Tiffins is a special restaurant at Walt Disney World because it is an ode to the Imagineers who created Disney's Animal Kingdom and documents their adventures in discovering stories to share across the Park. The rooms of this restaurant tell beautiful tales. The food is also beautiful, and each dish is a work of art. This Bread Service is served on a three-tiered tray that towers above the table. If you don't have a serving tray like this at home, no worries: Bowls and plates will do!

SERVES 2

For Coconut Lime Sauce
- ¼ cup coconut yogurt
- 1 tablespoon coconut cream
- 1 small lime, zested and juiced
- 1 teaspoon dried cilantro
- 1 teaspoon agave syrup
- ⅛ teaspoon cayenne pepper
- ¼ teaspoon salt
- ¼ teaspoon garlic powder

1. To make Coconut Lime Sauce: Whisk together all ingredients in a small bowl, then transfer to a small cup for serving.

(continued) ▶

For Ginger-Pear Chutney

2½ cups peeled, cored, and diced Bartlett pears
1 cup granulated sugar
1 tablespoon finely chopped crystalized ginger
½ cup apple cider vinegar
¼ teaspoon salt
¼ teaspoon ground cinnamon
¼ teaspoon ground allspice
¼ teaspoon ground cloves

For Assembly

2 Hawaiian rolls
3 pieces prepared pão de queijo
3 pieces prepared pappadam
¼ cup guava jam

2. To make Ginger-Pear Chutney: In a large pot or Dutch oven over medium heat, combine all ingredients and bring to a boil, stirring frequently. Reduce heat to medium-low and simmer uncovered 1–2 hours until mixture thickens. Remove from heat and scoop ¼ cup into a small cup. (Leftovers can be refrigerated up to 4 days.)
3. To Assemble: Place Coconut Lime Sauce next to Hawaiian rolls, Ginger-Pear Chutney next to the pappadam pieces, and pão de queijo next to the guava jam. Serve immediately.

Mix It Up

Guava jam may be tough to come by; if you can't get it (or don't prefer it), try some other options. Good substitutions are fig, peach, orange, or pineapple jam.

Lobster Nachos

···· **Lamplight Lounge, Disney California Adventure** ····

The most innovative of chefs find ways to use more parts of meats and vegetables, and the chefs of Lamplight Lounge are no exception. In recent years, they changed the composition of the Lobster Nachos to be sprinkled with lobster leg and claw meat instead of the more expensive tail meat. Just as tasty but more affordable, leg and claw meat goes great on these nachos. If you have easier access to lobster tail meat (or even imitation lobster meat), feel free to substitute those instead!

SERVES 2

- 2 frozen cooked whole lobsters, thawed
- ½ cup sour cream
- 1 tablespoon lime juice
- 1 tablespoon chipotle hot sauce
- ¼ teaspoon salt
- 3 cups tortilla chips
- ½ cup canned black beans, drained and rinsed
- ½ cup shredded aged Cheddar cheese
- ¼ cup Oaxaca cheese sauce
- ½ cup shredded Mexican cheese blend
- ¼ cup pico de gallo
- ¼ cup sliced serranos

1. Preheat oven to 425°F. Wrap lobsters individually in aluminum foil and place on a baking sheet.
2. Bake lobsters 5–8 minutes until meat is heated through. Allow to cool 10 minutes, then carefully extract and shred meat from the claws and legs of the lobsters and set aside. Eat or discard remaining lobster parts. Switch oven to broil on high.
3. Combine sour cream, lime juice, chipotle hot sauce, and salt in a small bowl.
4. To assemble, lay tortilla chips on a large broiler-safe platter. Top chips with black beans, Cheddar, Oaxaca cheese sauce, and shredded cheese. Place in oven to broil 1–2 minutes until cheese melts.
5. Remove from oven and pile on lobster meat, pico de gallo, and serranos and drizzle with sour cream mixture. Serve immediately.

······· **CHAPTER 6** ·······

Main Dishes

What's for dinner tonight? You *could* choose something basic to make for the family (the same ol' spaghetti in your meal rotation), *or* you could wow them with a Disney Parks favorite from a past or future trip. Dinner is the perfect time to take a trip down memory lane or prepare for an upcoming adventure. Either way, the recipes ahead beat out frozen chicken nuggets every time.

   Will you be making high-end cuisine tonight from Club 33 or Cinderella's Royal Table? Or going a bit more casual—but no less delicious—with out-of-this-planet eats from Docking Bay 7 Food and Cargo or Satu'li Canteen? Get fancy with Cranberry Roasted Medallion of Angus Beef Filet, or create a laid-back spread with Pork on Pork Burgers and the Parmesan Chips from Chapter 5. Whatever you are in the mood for, you'll be bringing the magic of the Disney Parks to your table.

Plaza Inn Specialty Chicken

······ **Plaza Inn, Disneyland** ······

This fried chicken platter has been a fan favorite at Disneyland for many, many years. Guests start lining up early to grab this cafeteria-style grub. And there is good reason: It's delicious! The batter delivers a great crunch. Serve with mashed potatoes, gravy, a biscuit, and vegetables for a meal that is big enough to share. If you grab a seat outside, you may even catch a parade coming down Main Street, U.S.A., that you can view from your seat!

SERVES 2

- 2 (6-ounce) skin-on, bone-in chicken thighs
- 2 (6-ounce) skin-on, bone-in chicken drumsticks
- 2 (4-ounce) skin-on, bone-in chicken wings
- 1 pint buttermilk
- 24 ounces peanut oil, for frying
- 2 cups all-purpose flour
- ½ cup cornstarch
- 1 tablespoon salt
- 1 tablespoon paprika
- 2 teaspoons onion powder
- 2 teaspoons garlic powder
- 1 teaspoon dried oregano
- 1 teaspoon dried basil
- 1 teaspoon ground white pepper
- ½ teaspoon cayenne pepper

1. Place chicken pieces in a large bowl and pour in buttermilk to coat. Cover with plastic wrap and refrigerate 4 hours up to overnight.
2. Pour oil in a large skillet so oil is about 1" deep. Preheat over medium heat to 350°F. Line a plate with paper towels.
3. Place all remaining ingredients in a large zip-top bag. Use tongs to remove 1 chicken piece from buttermilk and place into bag. Shake to coat. Remove chicken from bag and carefully place in preheated oil. Repeat with remaining chicken, frying half the pieces at a time. Fry about 15 minutes, flipping halfway through, or until pieces reach an internal temperature of 165°F.
4. Transfer to prepared plate. Allow to rest 10 minutes, then serve.

Disney Parks Tip

Sometimes the Plaza Inn has a special dining option, where you get a meal and a ticket to reserved seating for the nighttime parade. Just check the Disneyland app under "Dining Reservations" to see if there are any available during your trip!

Jambalaya

French Market Restaurant, Disneyland

Making this Jambalaya at home will make you feel as if you're right on the bayou! Tiana would be proud. And just like Tiana, feel free to play around with the spices in this dish to create your own ideal Jambalaya. Not into spicy food? Replace the andouille sausage with a plain beef sausage. Want more spice? Shake in as much cayenne pepper as you can handle! Serve with a corn bread muffin on the side for the full Park experience.

SERVES 6

- 2 teaspoons olive oil
- 1 (5-ounce) boneless, skinless chicken thigh, cut into 1" squares
- 1 medium green bell pepper, seeded and diced
- 2 medium andouille chicken sausages, sliced
- 1 teaspoon minced garlic
- ¾ cup chicken broth
- 1 (10-ounce) can crushed tomatoes, including juices
- 8 ounces raw jumbo shrimp, peeled and deveined
- 1 teaspoon salt
- 2 teaspoons Creole seasoning
- 6 cups prepared yellow rice
- 6 teaspoons chopped fresh parsley

1. In a large saucepan over medium heat, add oil and heat 2 minutes. Add chicken, bell pepper, sausages, and garlic. Cook 5–8 minutes until chicken is browned on the outside.
2. Add broth and tomatoes and allow to come to a boil. Stir in shrimp, salt, and Creole seasoning. Reduce heat to low, cover, and simmer about 10 minutes or until shrimp and chicken are cooked through (shrimp internal temperature to 120°F and chicken to 165°F).
3. To serve, scoop 1 cup yellow rice into a bowl, pile on the stew, and top with 1 teaspoon fresh parsley. Repeat to make six servings.

Battered & Fried Monte Cristo

••••• **Cafe Orleans, Disneyland** •••••

A Cafe Orleans favorite, the Monte Cristo sandwich has gained a hefty following and has even expanded to other locations, like The Plaza Restaurant at Magic Kingdom and Smokejumpers Grill at Disney California Adventure. But there's a special nostalgia to savoring your Monte Cristo at an outdoor table of Cafe Orleans. Serve with the Pomme Frites recipe in Chapter 5.

SERVES 1

48 ounces vegetable oil, for frying

1½ cups all-purpose flour

1 tablespoon baking powder

½ teaspoon salt

1⅓ cups water

1 large egg

2 slices white bread

2 thin slices Swiss cheese

2 thin slices deli turkey meat

2 thin slices deli ham meat

2 tablespoons confectioners' sugar

2 tablespoons strawberry jam

1. Pour oil into a large saucepan over medium heat and preheat to 375°F. Line a plate with paper towels.
2. Whisk together flour, baking powder, salt, water, and egg in a medium bowl. Add more water as needed until batter is dip-able.
3. Lay cheese, turkey, and ham on 1 slice bread and top with second slice. Use two toothpicks to keep the sandwich together during frying. Carefully dip entire sandwich into prepared batter until covered and gently shake off excess. Carefully place battered sandwich into hot oil and cook 2–5 minutes until batter is brown and crispy. Transfer to prepared plate to cool 5 minutes.
4. To serve, remove toothpicks and slice sandwich in half, top to bottom. Sift confectioners' sugar over sandwich and serve with strawberry jam on the side for dipping.

Herb-Salted Pork Tenderloin

Be Our Guest Restaurant, Magic Kingdom

Served at the impeccably themed Be Our Guest Restaurant, Herb-Salted Pork Tenderloin will have you singing along with Lumière. At Be Our Guest Restaurant, this dish is also served with crispy pork belly, seasonal vegetables, and candied pecans. If you want the authentic experiences, add these to your plate! If you'd rather make your own symphony of flavors, add whichever sides you would like.

SERVES 4

- 3 teaspoons minced garlic
- 1 teaspoon dried basil
- 1 teaspoon dried thyme
- 1 teaspoon dried rosemary
- 1 teaspoon ground black pepper
- 1 teaspoon salt
- 2 tablespoons olive oil
- 1 (1–2 pound) pork tenderloin

1. Preheat oven to 400°F. Grease a 9" × 13" glass or ceramic baking dish with nonstick cooking spray.
2. In a small bowl, mix together garlic, basil, thyme, rosemary, pepper, salt, and olive oil. Lay pork tenderloin in prepared baking dish and rub with herbed spread.
3. Bake 30–40 minutes until the internal temperature of the pork is 145°F. Remove from oven and allow to rest 10 minutes in baking dish.
4. Slice into 1"-thick slices and serve.

Tenderloin of Beef

Cinderella's Royal Table, Magic Kingdom

This absolutely melt-in-your-mouth tenderloin is sure to disappear long before the clock strikes twelve, so grab your magic wand (and magic spoon) and get cooking! Served with seasonal vegetables and whipped potatoes in the Park, you can do the same at home. Check and see what vegetables are in season and are sold at your local grocery store or farmers' market. Then prepare and serve alongside this never-out-of-season Tenderloin of Beef. Cinderella's Royal Table is actually *inside* of Cinderella Castle at Magic Kingdom and offers a special invitation to see inside the otherwise closed building.

SERVES 1

1 tablespoon Montreal steak seasoning
1 teaspoon dried parsley
1 teaspoon dried rosemary
1 (½-pound) beef tenderloin steak
1 teaspoon salted butter
1 large shallot, peeled and diced
½ teaspoon salt
½ cup dry red wine
1 cup beef stock
½ teaspoon ground black pepper
1 tablespoon olive oil

1. Mix Montreal steak seasoning, parsley, and rosemary in a small bowl. Pat steak dry with a paper towel. Rub seasoning mixture all over steak and allow to sit at room temperature 30 minutes.
2. Melt butter in a medium skillet over medium-low heat. Add shallot and salt, then cook 10 minutes. Add red wine and reduce 5 minutes. Add in beef stock and pepper and reduce until slightly thick, about 10 minutes. Set aside.
3. Preheat a cast iron skillet over high heat 5 minutes. Add olive oil, then carefully place steak into pan. Cook without flipping about 3 minutes or until steak easily releases from pan. Flip and cook another 3 minutes. Internal temperature should be 145°F for medium doneness. Remove from heat and transfer steak to a plate to allow to rest 10 minutes.
4. Move steak to a dining plate. Drizzle wine sauce over steak and serve immediately.

Curry-Spiced Pizza

····· **Connections Eatery, EPCOT** ·····

It's an uncommon lineup of ingredients for a pizza, but somehow it just *works*. It is like a whole container of Indian takeout on top of a crust: What could be better than that? Connections Eatery replaced what used to be Innoventions at EPCOT and boasts a huge dining room with lots of air-conditioned seating available. Be sure to check out the massive mural on the wall. Stretching over 160 feet long, it depicts people from around the world harvesting and using food and beverage staples from their regions, illustrating how these foods "connect" us all together.

YIELDS 2 PIZZAS

For Pizza Crust
- 1 cup warm water (110°F)
- 1 teaspoon rapid-rise yeast
- 1 teaspoon olive oil
- 1¼ cups all-purpose flour

For Pizza Toppings
- 1 cup water
- 4 small Yukon Gold potatoes, peeled and cubed
- 1 (16-ounce) jar tikka masala sauce
- 1 cup diced carrots
- 1 cup diced Roma tomatoes
- 1 cup frozen peas
- 2 cups plant-based mozzarella cheese
- ½ cup plain Greek yogurt
- 1 tablespoon lime juice
- 1 cup fresh cilantro

1. To make Pizza Crust: In a large bowl, mix water, yeast, olive oil, and flour with your hands until just combined and dough is shaggy. Cover with a clean towel and let sit 15 minutes.
2. Grease two large bowls with nonstick cooking spray.
3. After 15 minutes, knead dough by hand 3 minutes or until dough is well combined and soft. Cut into two equal-sized pieces and place each piece in a prepared bowl. Cover with a tea towel and let rise in a warm place 1 hour.
4. To make Pizza Toppings: In a medium microwave-safe bowl, add water and potato cubes. Microwave 5 minutes or until fork-tender. Remove, drain, and set aside.
5. In a medium saucepan over medium heat, combine tikka masala sauce, carrots, cooked potatoes, and tomatoes. Bring to a boil, reduce heat to low, and cook 5–10 minutes until carrots are soft. Add in peas and cook an additional 3 minutes. Remove from heat.

(continued) ▶

6. Place a full-sized baking sheet into oven and preheat oven to 550°F.
7. Turn each dough ball out onto a clean surface. Coat your hands in olive oil and carefully push each ball into a flat, round crust.
8. Scoop about 1 cup topping sauce and vegetables onto each Pizza Crust and spread evenly. Sprinkle each Pizza with 1 cup cheese. Bake Pizzas one at a time 5–7 minutes, until Pizza Crust is brown and cheese is melted. Remove from oven and allow to cool 10 minutes.
9. Mix yogurt and lime juice together. Cut Pizzas into slices and drizzle each slice with lime yogurt sauce. Garnish each slice with a sprig of fresh cilantro. Serve immediately.

Disney Parks Tip

Right next to Connections Eatery is the groundbreaking attraction Guardians of the Galaxy: Cosmic Rewind. This experience teams you up with the Guardians and Nova Corps to get the Cosmic Generator back. If those words mean nothing to you, don't worry: You can just enjoy a thrilling ride through space while jamming out to one of six popular rock songs!

Cranberry Roasted Medallion of Angus Beef Filet

······ **Club 33, Disneyland** ······

Club 33 is the most exclusive dining establishment at Disneyland bar none. You can gain entry only if you are a member of Club 33 or have been invited by a member. Menus are seasonal and ever-changing by the in-house chefs. Enjoy this Cranberry Roasted Medallion of Angus Beef Filet at home whenever you want, no membership or reservation needed! Serve with local root vegetables.

SERVES 2

- 2 (1/3-pound) cuts filet mignon
- 1 teaspoon salt
- 1 teaspoon ground black pepper
- 2 tablespoons salted butter
- 1 cup jellied cranberry
- 2 tablespoons pure maple syrup
- 2 tablespoons ketchup
- 2 tablespoons apple cider vinegar

1. Allow cuts of filet mignon to rest at room temperature 20 minutes. Season all sides with salt and pepper.
2. Heat a medium grill pan over high heat and add butter. Cook steaks 2–3 minutes per side until internal temperature reaches 140°F. Remove pan from heat and transfer meat to a plate to rest 10 minutes.
3. Combine jellied cranberry, maple syrup, ketchup, and apple cider vinegar in a small saucepan over medium heat. Bring to a boil, then remove from heat.
4. Assemble two plates with 1 piece of filet mignon each and drizzle generously with cranberry sauce. Serve.

Vegetable Korma

Sunshine Seasons, EPCOT

Replacing animal meats with plant-based meats is becoming increasingly popular. It is actually environmentally conscious to do so; swapping out more animal meats for plant ones could add years to our planet's life. More and more companies have been creating and tweaking plant-based meats and have truly perfected the texture and flavor to mimic that of animal meats. This dish is no exception; the Gardein Chick'n Strips taste and look just like real chicken!

SERVES 6

- 1½ tablespoons vegetable oil
- 1 medium yellow onion, peeled and sliced
- 1 teaspoon minced ginger
- 4 teaspoons minced garlic
- 4 large carrots, peeled and sliced into 3" sticks
- 3 tablespoons unsalted cashews
- 1 (4-ounce) can tomato sauce
- 1 (10-ounce) bag Gardein Chick'n Strips
- 2 teaspoons salt
- 1½ tablespoons curry powder
- 1 cup frozen peas
- 1 medium green bell pepper, seeded and cut into strips
- 1 cup unsweetened almond milk
- 6 cups prepared white rice

1. In a large skillet or wok over medium heat, add oil and allow to preheat 2 minutes. Add onion and cook 5 minutes while stirring until soft and translucent. Add ginger and garlic and cook 1 minute more. Add carrots, cashews, tomato sauce, Gardein Chick'n Strips, salt, and curry powder. Cook and stir frequently 10 minutes.
2. Add peas, bell pepper, and almond milk. Cover and reduce heat to low and simmer 10 minutes or until carrots are soft.
3. Scoop into six dishes with 1 cup white rice each and serve immediately.

Savoyarde Galette

La Crêperie de Paris, EPCOT

Tucked in the very back of the France pavilion at EPCOT, La Crêperie de Paris is a quaint restaurant with a small dining room and a lovely French café vibe. Servers wear iconic black-and-white-striped shirts and deliver incredible crepes to your table. The Savoyarde is one of their most popular options, and it is no wonder why. Savory ingredients piled up in a buckwheat crepe make for a hearty and tasty meal you can enjoy any time of day.

SERVES 6

For Caramelized Onions
- 1 teaspoon olive oil
- 1 medium yellow onion, peeled and cut into strips
- 1 teaspoon salt
- 1 teaspoon granulated sugar

For Crepes
- 1 cup buckwheat flour
- 2 large eggs
- ½ cup whole milk
- ½ teaspoon salt
- 2 tablespoons salted butter, melted

For Assembly
- 3 cups shredded raclette cheese
- 18 strips cooked bacon
- 1 pound Bayonne ham or prosciutto

1. **To make Caramelized Onions:** Place oil in a large skillet over medium-high heat. Add onion slices and stir to coat. Reduce heat to medium and allow to cook, stirring occasionally, 10 minutes.
2. Sprinkle on salt and sugar and stir to coat. Allow to cook 30 minutes or until deep brown but not burned, then remove from heat and set aside.
3. **To make Crepes:** In a blender, add all ingredients and pulse until well combined, about 1 minute.
4. Preheat an electric crepe pan or a large skillet to medium-high heat. Spray pan or skillet with nonstick cooking spray. Pouring directly from blender, swirl about ¼–½ cup batter in pan to evenly coat the bottom. Cook about 2 minutes, then slide a spatula around outside edges and flip to cook opposite side 2 minutes more. Transfer to a large plate and repeat with remaining batter. Excess batter or cooked Crepes can be kept covered in the refrigerator up to 1 week.
5. **To Assemble:** Lay 1 Crepe on center of a large plate. Sprinkle with ½ cup raclette cheese. Scoop in ¼ cup Caramelized Onions and lay on 3 strips of bacon. Fold in sides of Crepe to the middle to create a square. Lay several thin slices of ham or prosciutto on top of Crepe. Repeat with remaining Crepes and ingredients. Serve immediately.

Pork on Pork Burger

Sci-Fi Dine-In Theater Restaurant, Disney's Hollywood Studios

This is not just a pork burger, this is a Pork on Pork Burger! A juicy pork patty topped with a thick slab of roasted pork belly. Sci-Fi Dine-In Theater Restaurant shows old-fashioned 1950s science-fiction flicks on the big screen, with thrilling titles like *Cat-Women of the Moon*, *The Amazing Colossal Man*, and *The Horror of Party Beach*. While these might not be the kind of shows you are used to watching today, they are sure entertaining for a meal at Disney's Hollywood Studios. If you want to have this experience at home, you can watch those movies on *YouTube* while you eat.

SERVES 1

For Caramelized Onions
- 2 tablespoons olive oil
- ¼ cup yellow onion slices
- 1 teaspoon salt

For Carolina Mustard Sauce
- ⅓ cup yellow mustard
- ¼ cup honey
- 2 tablespoons light brown sugar
- ¼ cup apple cider vinegar
- 1 tablespoon ketchup
- 1 teaspoon Worcestershire sauce
- ½ teaspoon garlic powder
- ⅛ teaspoon cayenne pepper

1. To make Caramelized Onions: In a large pan over medium heat, add olive oil and allow to heat 3 minutes. Add onion slices and stir. Stir occasionally 10 minutes. Add salt. Keep stirring occasionally until onions have softened and browned, about 45 minutes. Remove from heat.
2. To make Carolina Mustard Sauce: Place all ingredients in a small saucepan and bring to a boil over medium heat, stirring frequently. Reduce heat to low and simmer 10 minutes. Remove from heat and allow to cool at room temperature 1 hour. Pour into a jar, cover, and refrigerate.
3. To make Roasted Pork Belly: Preheat oven to 450°F.
4. Pat pork belly dry with a paper towel and sprinkle with salt, sugar, and pepper. Place on a baking sheet (fat side up) and roast 15 minutes. Reduce heat to 275°F and roast an additional 30 minutes, or until internal temperature reaches 155°F; remove from oven. Set aside.

For Roasted Pork Belly

⅛ pound pork belly
½ teaspoon salt
½ teaspoon granulated sugar
⅛ teaspoon ground black pepper

For Pork Patty

¼ pound ground pork
¼ teaspoon salt
¼ teaspoon ground black pepper
⅛ teaspoon ground sage

For Assembly

1 tablespoon salted butter, softened
1 hamburger bun
1 slice white sharp Cheddar cheese
¼ cup tricolor coleslaw

5. **To make Pork Patty:** Combine ingredients in a medium bowl. Roll into a ball and pat into a disk about 4" wide and 1" thick. Press your fingers into the center to make an indent.

6. Preheat a grill pan to medium-high heat for 3 minutes. Place Patty on grill pan and cook without flipping 5–6 minutes until underside is browned. Flip and cook an additional 4–6 minutes until internal temperature reaches 160°F. Remove to a plate to rest 10 minutes.

7. **To Assemble:** Spread softened butter on insides of bun top and bottom and place on still-hot grill pan. Cook 1–2 minutes until butter browns. Remove from heat.

8. Lay down bun bottom on a serving plate. Add Pork Patty, cheese, Caramelized Onions, Roasted Pork Belly, tricolor slaw, 1 tablespoon Carolina Mustard Sauce, and bun top. Serve immediately.

Slow-Roasted Sliced Grilled Beef Bowls

Satu'li Canteen, Disney's Animal Kingdom

This is the perfect dish for a day at Disney or just hanging out at home! Noodles, vegetables, beef, sauce, and boba balls create a whole meal in one bowl. If you don't have boba balls on hand, you can easily order them from online retailers. Or you can omit them entirely. They add a little kick to the dish but are otherwise mostly used to create a special space-y accoutrement becoming of a dish served on the planet of Pandora.

SERVES 4

- 1 tablespoon minced garlic
- 1 teaspoon ground cayenne pepper
- 1 teaspoon salt
- 1 tablespoon dried rosemary
- 1 tablespoon dried thyme
- 1 teaspoon dried oregano
- 1 tablespoon dried basil
- ½ cup red wine vinegar
- 1 (3–4-pound) boneless rump roast
- 4 cups prepared stir-fry noodles
- 4 cups tricolor coleslaw
- 4 tablespoons smokey chipotle boba balls
- 1 cup creamy herb salad dressing

1. In a large zip-top bag, combine garlic, cayenne pepper, salt, rosemary, thyme, oregano, basil, and red wine vinegar. Add roast to bag, seal, and refrigerate 30 minutes up to overnight.
2. Preheat an outdoor grill to medium-high heat on one side of grill.
3. Remove roast from marinade and place on other side of grill away from direct heat. Shut lid and cook 1–3 hours (depending on shape of roast) until internal temperature reaches 145°F.
4. Transfer to a large plate and allow to rest 20 minutes. Slice as thinly as possible into 1"–2" pieces and set aside.
5. Assemble bowls with 1 cup cooked noodles, ½ cup sliced beef, 1 cup slaw, and 1 tablespoon boba balls each, then drizzle with creamy herb dressing. Serve immediately.

Felucian Kefta and Hummus Garden Spread

.... **Docking Bay 7 Food and Cargo, Disney's Hollywood Studios** ....
and Disneyland

Get into your hunk of junk and make your grocery run in 12 parsecs or less, because all the citizens of Batuu are going to be grabbing these ingredients off the shelves once they hear about this incredible recipe! It doesn't even take a Jedi master to get this meal on the table. Try making the Tomato Cucumber Relish and Herb Hummus ahead of time and simply warm the meatless meatballs right before serving.

SERVES 4

For Tomato Cucumber Relish

1 large English cucumber, diced
3 medium Roma tomatoes, diced
2 tablespoons olive oil
1 tablespoon balsamic glaze
1 teaspoon dried oregano
1 teaspoon salt
¼ teaspoon ground black pepper

For Herb Hummus

1 (15-ounce) can chickpeas, drained
1 teaspoon minced garlic
2 tablespoons tahini
2 tablespoons fresh parsley
2 tablespoons minced fresh basil leaves

1. To make Tomato Cucumber Relish: Toss together all ingredients in a medium bowl, cover, and refrigerate 30 minutes.
2. To make Herb Hummus: Add all ingredients to a food processor or blender and blend 2 minutes. Scrape down sides and blend 1 minute more or until mixture is smooth. Scoop into a medium bowl and set aside.

(continued) ▶

- 3 tablespoons chopped green onions
- 3 tablespoons lemon juice
- ½ teaspoon salt
- ⅓ cup olive oil

For Assembly

- 1 (12.7-ounce) bag Gardein Plant-Based Meatballs, prepared
- 1 pita bread, quartered
- 4 stems microgreens

3. To Assemble: Spread ¼ Herb Hummus into a serving bowl. Top with 3 meatballs and scoop 2 tablespoons Tomato Cucumber Relish on top of meatballs. Place 1 pita bread quarter into side of bowl and garnish meatballs with 1 stem of microgreens. Repeat with remaining ingredients to make four servings and serve immediately. Leftover hummus and relish can be covered and refrigerated up to 1 week.

Serving Suggestion

You can serve this like they do at Docking Bay 7, as an entrée, or you can serve it as an appetizer for a crowd! Simply separate each of the ingredients and allow guests to pile what they want on their plates and use the pitas to scoop up their choices like dips.

St. Louis Rib Dinners

···· **Flame Tree Barbecue, Disney's Animal Kingdom** ····

Everyone needs a go-to rib recipe on hand for feeding a crowd some barbecue. This delicious and easy-to-put-together meal can be your new favorite for whenever the craving strikes. If you are making these for just one person instead of a crowd, place any extra leftovers in a zip-top bag in the refrigerator up to four days. Then you can have a couple of ribs a day for lunch! Flame Tree Barbecue serves its ribs with beans and coleslaw.

SERVES 4

- 1 cup honey barbecue sauce
- 1 teaspoon salt
- 2 teaspoons ground black pepper
- 2 tablespoons paprika
- 1 tablespoon garlic powder
- 1 tablespoon dried oregano
- 2 tablespoons brown sugar
- 1 (3–4-pound) slab St. Louis ribs

1. Preheat oven to 350°F. Line a baking sheet with aluminum foil.
2. Combine barbecue sauce, salt, pepper, paprika, garlic powder, oregano, and brown sugar in a medium bowl. Pour and smooth sauce over entire slab of ribs. Place ribs on prepared baking sheet, cover loosely with foil, and bake 2 hours. Remove foil from top of ribs and bake 20 minutes more. Remove from oven.
3. Cut into individual ribs and serve immediately.

Hot Link Bowls

Harambe Market, Disney's Animal Kingdom

It has been a top goal of Disney chefs to provide inclusive dining, and that includes dishes with no meat or animal products. This Hot Link Bowl recipe is one of the many vegan dishes served at Disney Parks. If you have a food allergy or particular food lifestyle choice, simply use the Disneyland or Walt Disney World app to check the menu for the restaurant where you want to dine.

SERVES 6

- 4 tablespoons vegetable oil, divided
- 1½ cups long-grain rice
- 1 teaspoon minced garlic
- 2¼ cups water
- 1 teaspoon salt
- 3 tablespoons lime juice
- 1 cup chopped fresh cilantro
- 6 plant-based "sausage" hot links
- 3 cups mixed greens
- 1½ cups pico de gallo salsa

1. In a medium saucepan over medium heat, add 2 tablespoons oil. Add in rice and stir to coat in oil and toast about 3 minutes. Add in garlic and cook 1 minute more.
2. Add in water and salt, stir to combine, and bring to a boil. Cover and reduce heat to low and cook without stirring 15 minutes. Remove from heat but keep lid on 8 minutes more. Fluff rice with a fork and stir in lime juice and chopped cilantro. Set aside.
3. In a medium skillet over medium heat, add remaining 2 tablespoons oil. Add hot links and flip and cook about 10 minutes or until outsides are browned. Remove from heat.
4. Build your bowls by placing a scoop of cilantro rice into a bowl, topping with ½ cup mixed greens and ¼ cup pico de gallo, and finishing with 1 hot link per bowl. Serve immediately.

Mix It Up!

At Disney, they only serve this dish with hot plant-based sausage. But at home, if you'd rather have a non-spicy beef dog in your bowl instead, have at it! Both are totally delicious and create a new flavor profile of the same dish with a quick switch.

Beef Bulgogi Burritos

Lucky Fortune Cookery, Disney California Adventure

This burrito is quickly becoming one of the most popular food items at Disney California Adventure, so you'll want to place a mobile order for one to ensure you get your hands on it in the Park! Luckily, you don't have to clamor for one of these burritos at home; you can just whip one up whenever you like. In fact, you'd better start marinating your beef now, because you're probably going to want one ASAP! The Lucky Fortune Cookery is in the Pacific Wharf area of Disney California Adventure, which is like a large food court full of different Californian flavors that all share one big outdoor seating area. The restaurant serves these burritos with garlic-flavored chips.

SERVES 6

- ¼ cup soy sauce
- ¼ cup freeze-dried chopped green onions
- 2½ tablespoons granulated sugar
- 2 tablespoons minced garlic
- 2 tablespoons sesame oil
- ½ teaspoon ground black pepper
- 1 pound flank steak, thinly sliced
- 6 large flour tortillas
- 6 cups prepared white rice
- 3 cups tricolor coleslaw

1. In a large zip-top bag, add soy sauce, green onions, sugar, garlic, oil, and pepper. Massage to combine. Pour ½ cup sauce in a small bowl, cover, and refrigerate. Add flank steak strips to bag, seal, and refrigerate 4 hours up to overnight.
2. Preheat an outdoor grill or grill pan on high heat 5 minutes. Remove steak pieces with tongs and grill 1–2 minutes per side until internal temperature reaches 130°F. Remove from grill and allow to rest 10 minutes.
3. Lay out tortillas on serving plates and add 1 cup rice and ½ cup coleslaw to each tortilla. Drizzle 1–2 tablespoons reserved sauce onto rice and coleslaw. Add in ⅙ of the steak to each tortilla, fold, and wrap tightly into a burrito. Cut in half and serve.

Impossible Spoonful

Pym Test Kitchen, Disney California Adventure

At Pym Test Kitchen, this dish is served in an enormous metal ladle, and the giant meatball on top feels even larger than it is because they place a tiny fork in it! Everything is weird sized at Pym's, so of course this dish is no exception. Usually, a pasta dish at home is served with uniformly sized noodles, but not here! The playfulness is super fun, and your kids will get a kick out of it when you tell them some of the noodles got huge and some of them shrunk!

SERVES 2

- 1 cup rigatoni pasta
- 1 cup ditalini pasta
- 1 tablespoon olive oil
- 2 cups marinara sauce
- 2 large frozen plant-based meatballs, thawed
- ½ cup dairy-free Parmesan cheese
- 2 tablespoons micro basil

1. Cook rigatoni and ditalini pastas according to package labels. Remove from heat and drain.
2. Heat olive oil in a large skillet and pour drained pastas into skillet. Add marinara sauce and meatballs. Cook about 5 minutes, or until sauce is warmed and meatballs are warm all the way through.
3. Scoop into two bowls, making sure each has a large meatball on top. Sprinkle each with dairy-free Parmesan and micro basil.

Ka-Cheeseburger

····· **Flo's V8 Cafe, Disney California Adventure** ·····

Take the detour off Route 66 to Flo's V8 Cafe, where hot food and cold milkshakes are served up to hungry travelers on their way across the country…or Disney California Adventure. When you're making this burger at home, try to get as artistic as Ramone and customize it however you like! Instead of chrome rims and white-wall wheels, condiments and toppings are your medium. For the full Flo's V8 Cafe experience, serve with steak fries, a pickle spear, some iceberg lettuce, and a slice of beefsteak tomato on the side.

SERVES 1

- 1 tablespoon olive oil
- ¼ medium yellow onion, peeled and sliced
- 1½ teaspoons salt, divided
- 1 (⅓-pound) lean beef steak burger patty
- ½ teaspoon ground black pepper
- 1 sesame seed hamburger bun
- 1 slice sharp Cheddar cheese
- 1 tablespoon Thousand Island dressing

1. In a large pan over medium heat, add olive oil and allow to heat 3 minutes. Add onion slices and stir occasionally 10 minutes. Add 1 teaspoon salt. Lower the heat to medium-low and keep stirring occasionally until onions have softened and browned, about 45 minutes. Remove from heat.
2. Sprinkle both sides of burger patty with remaining ½ teaspoon salt and pepper. In a medium pan over medium heat, grease pan with nonstick cooking spray. Add burger patty and cook 7–8 minutes until internal temperature reaches 160°F, flipping halfway through. Remove from heat.
3. To assemble, layer hamburger bun bottom with burger patty, slice of cheese, caramelized onions, and Thousand Island Dressing and finish with bun top. Serve.

CHAPTER 7

Desserts

It's the moment so many of us are waiting for: dessert! Desserts are a fan favorite at Disney Parks (don't we want to allow ourselves a sweet treat or three while on vacation?)—but don't let being at home stop you from treating yourself; you deserve it!

This chapter has all the yummy goodies you look forward to each time you visit Disney Parks. And now you won't have to order extra Celestial-Sized Candy Bars to stuff in your backpack to take home with you; you've got the recipe right here in this book and can make them any time you like! What will *you* make first? The famous Wookiee Cookies? Or how about the iconic Ooey Gooey Toffee Cake? Or maybe newer Park delights like Fried Wontons or Vegan Blackberry Cupcakes? Anything you whip up is sure to be magical!

Mine Cart Brownies

.... **Jolly Holiday Bakery Cafe, Disneyland** ....

One of the most adorable treats served at the Disney Parks, the Mine Cart Brownie looks exactly like you'd hope—including little wheels and gleaming gems. And the best thing is all the ingredients are easy to find and don't require extra molds or materials. In 2021, Disneyland debuted the new ride Snow White's Enchanted Wish, a reimagining of the 1955 opening day attraction Snow White's Scary Adventures. Riders get to jump into mine carts and experience the story of Snow White up close and personal.

SERVES 10

- 1 cup salted butter
- 1 cup semisweet chocolate chips
- 2 cups granulated sugar
- 2 teaspoons vanilla extract
- 5 large eggs
- 1/3 cup unsweetened cocoa powder
- 2/3 cup all-purpose flour
- 1/2 teaspoon salt
- 14 tablespoons white frosting, divided
- 2 teaspoons each blue, white, yellow, red, and green sugar sprinkles
- 40 milk chocolate candy melt circles

1. Preheat oven to 350°F. Line a 9" × 13" baking dish with parchment paper.
2. In a large microwave-safe bowl, add butter and chocolate chips. Microwave on high 30 seconds. Stir. Continue microwaving in 30-second increments and stirring until chocolate is melted. Allow to cool 30 minutes.
3. Stir in sugar, vanilla, eggs, cocoa powder, flour, and salt until just combined and not lumpy. Pour batter into prepared baking dish and bake 40–50 minutes until a knife inserted in the center comes out clean. Allow to cool in pan 1 hour.
4. Once completely cool, invert entire pan onto a baking sheet and remove parchment paper. Cut into ten rectangles. Flip and spread the top of each rectangle with 1 tablespoon frosting. Mix all sprinkles together in a small bowl and sprinkle over frosting. With remaining 13 tablespoons frosting, dab a small amount on the back of chocolate candy melts and place like wheels around sides of rectangles, 4 for each rectangle. Serve.

Sweet Lumpia!

The Tropical Hideaway, Disneyland

The Tropical Hideaway is best known as the place to get Dole Whip desserts, from classic pineapple to seasonal flavors, and even loaded varieties! But once guests grab the Whip, they also love to get an order of Sweet Lumpia! for a warm bite to go with their cold soft serve. Featuring flavors of the Philippines, lumpia is a hand-held sweet that you can wrap anything up in and deep fry.

YIELDS 4 LUMPIA

- 48 ounces vegetable oil, for frying
- 4 spring roll pastry wrappers
- 1 medium ripe banana, peeled and sliced
- ¼ cup canned jackfruit, drained and cut into strips
- 4 tablespoons light brown sugar
- 2 tablespoons caramel syrup

1. Pour oil in a large shallow pot or deep fryer and preheat to 350°F. Line a plate with paper towels.
2. Lay 1 spring roll wrapper on a clean surface with one corner pointed toward you. Run a moistened finger along each of the wrapper edges. Place 3–4 banana slices in the middle of the wrapper, then 2 slices of jackfruit on top of banana. Sprinkle 1 tablespoon brown sugar onto jackfruit. Fold side corners over fruit in center and roll up like a burrito. Make sure all edges are well sealed. Repeat with remaining wrappers and fillings.
3. Carefully lower each lumpia one at a time into preheated oil and fry 2–4 minutes until golden brown. Transfer from oil to prepared plate to drain.
4. Place two rolls each on two plates and drizzle each roll with caramel syrup. Serve immediately.

Mix It Up!

This variety has banana and jackfruit inside, but while you have the fryer heated up, try filling some with other toppings! How about pineapple chunks, or cream cheese? When your kitchen is The Tropical Hideaway, you can make whatever you like.

House-Made Chocolate-Chunk Cookie Sundaes

.... **The Golden Horseshoe, Disneyland** ....

Ice cream with fresh-out-of-the-oven warm cookies drenched in your favorite toppings? Doesn't your mouth water just thinking of it? The Golden Horseshoe places a cookie on either side of a large scoop of ice cream to look like Mickey ears for a magical way to serve up a dessert. If you don't eat all the cookies right off (if you can resist), save the extras in a sealed container on the counter for up to one week. Then just pop two in the microwave on a plate for 20 seconds to heat up before placing them on your sundae. Hot and fresh yet again!

SERVES 4

1 cup salted butter
1 cup granulated sugar
1 cup light brown sugar
1 tablespoon vanilla extract
2 large eggs
1 teaspoon baking soda
1 teaspoon baking powder
½ teaspoon salt
2½ cups all-purpose flour
½ cup milk chocolate chips
½ cup dark chocolate chips

1. Preheat oven to 350°F. Line two full-sized baking sheets with parchment paper.
2. In a large skillet over medium heat, add butter and allow to melt completely. Continue cooking butter until color becomes a deep brown, about 5 minutes. Remove from heat and allow to cool 10 minutes.
3. In the bowl of a stand mixer fitted with paddle attachment, add browned butter, granulated sugar, brown sugar, and vanilla. Mix 1 minute on medium speed to combine. Add in eggs one at a time while continuing to mix. Add in baking soda, baking powder, and salt while continuing to mix. Add in flour ½ cup at a time until well combined. Add in milk, dark, and semisweet chocolate chips and mix until just incorporated.

- ½ cup semisweet chocolate chips
- 4 cups vanilla ice cream
- 1 cup canned whipped cream
- 4 tablespoons chocolate sauce
- 4 tablespoons caramel sauce
- 4 tablespoons rainbow sprinkles

4. Use a small cookie scoop to scoop dough onto prepared sheets. Leftover dough (or baked cookies) can be covered and refrigerated up to 1 week. Bake 10–12 minutes until sides are browned and middle is no longer wet. Remove from oven and allow cookies to cool completely on pan, about 1 hour.
5. To assemble sundaes, scoop 1 cup vanilla ice cream into each of four serving bowls. Top with whipped cream. Drizzle on chocolate and caramel sauces, then top with sprinkles. Add two cookies to either side of ice cream to mimic Mickey ears. Serve immediately.

Ooey Gooey Toffee Cake

Liberty Tree Tavern, Magic Kingdom

Ooey Gooey Toffee Cake certainly has a loyal following, and guests make reservations at Liberty Tree Tavern just to get some. Now you can enjoy it from the comfort of your own home and can pair it with any meal you'd like! Unlike most cakes, this one has a thicker bottom and a fluffy top, offering a range of exciting textures as you eat.

SERVES 12

For Bottom Layer
- 1 (15.25-ounce) box yellow cake mix
- 1 large egg
- ½ cup salted butter, softened
- ½ cup mini semisweet chocolate chips
- ½ cup toffee bits

For Top Layer
- 8 ounces cream cheese, softened
- 2 large eggs
- 2 teaspoons vanilla extract
- ¼ cup salted butter, softened
- 3½ cups confectioners' sugar
- ½ cup mini semisweet chocolate chips
- ½ cup toffee bits

For Assembly
- 12 cups vanilla ice cream
- 12 tablespoons chocolate sauce
- 12 teaspoons toffee bits

1. To make Bottom Layer: Preheat oven to 350°F. Grease twelve divots of jumbo-muffin tins with nonstick cooking spray.
2. In a medium bowl, add yellow cake mix, egg, butter, chocolate chips, and toffee bits. Stir until combined and no longer powdery. Divide evenly among twelve jumbo-muffin tin divots so that about ½" of each divot is filled. Set aside.
3. To make Top Layer: In the bowl of a stand mixer fitted with paddle attachment, add cream cheese, eggs, vanilla, and butter. Mix 1–2 minutes on medium speed until well combined. Slowly add in confectioners' sugar and mix 1 minute more. Fold in chocolate chips and toffee bits. Divide evenly among filled muffin tin divots, placing on top of Bottom Layer.
4. Bake 30–40 minutes until no longer wet in the middle. Allow to cool 30 minutes in pan.
5. To Assemble: Carefully slide a knife around the edges of the cakes to loosen from pan and gently remove each cake. Serve each cake topped with 1 cup vanilla ice cream, drizzled with 1 tablespoon chocolate sauce, and sprinkled with 1 teaspoon toffee bits.

Butterscotch Pudding

••••• **The Crystal Palace, Magic Kingdom** •••••

The Crystal Palace is a Signature Table Service restaurant featuring a generous buffet and all the friends from the Hundred Acre Wood coming around to say hello! Yes, Winnie the Pooh, Tigger, Piglet, Rabbit, and other friends may wander through the dining room to greet you as you eat. When you make this Butterscotch Pudding at home, you can do as Christopher Robin does and set up your stuffed animals to enjoy it with you.

SERVES 12

- 3 cups whole milk
- 4 large egg yolks
- 1½ cups light brown sugar
- ¼ cup cornstarch
- ½ teaspoon salt
- 2 tablespoons salted butter
- 2 cups prepared caramel popcorn

1. In a large nonstick pan over medium heat, add milk and egg yolks and stir well to combine. Add brown sugar, cornstarch, and salt and stir to combine. Continue stirring continuously while mixture thickens, about 10 minutes. Stir in butter until melted and remove from heat. Pour mixture through a medium sieve into a bowl and refrigerate 1 hour or until cool.
2. Once cooled, scoop mixture into twelve small cups. Any leftovers can be refrigerated up to 4 days. Top each serving with 3–4 caramel popcorn pieces and serve immediately.

The Sword in the Sweet

······ **Cinderella's Royal Table, Magic Kingdom** ······

You'll feel just like Arthur as you pull a cookie sword out of yummy pudding in this dessert! It's served as part of the kids' menu at Cinderella's Royal Table, but you don't have to be a little prince or princess to fall for this treat. In fact, it is just like The Grey Stuff served at Be Our Guest Restaurant in Beast's Castle. This variety comes with crumbly streusel topping.

SERVES 4

For Streusel Topping
½ cup cold salted butter
1½ cups all-purpose flour
½ cup light brown sugar
½ cup granulated sugar

For Sugar Cookie Sword
¾ cup salted butter, softened
1 cup granulated sugar
2 large eggs
1 teaspoon vanilla extract
2½ cups all-purpose flour
¼ teaspoon baking powder
¼ teaspoon baking soda
½ teaspoon salt

1. To make Streusel Topping: Preheat oven to 350°F. Line a baking sheet with parchment paper.
2. Place all ingredients in a medium bowl and use a pastry cutter or knife to cut the butter into small pieces until mix resembles coarse crumbs. Pour crumbs onto prepared baking sheet and bake 8–10 minutes until golden brown. Remove from oven and allow to cool completely, about 2 hours.
3. To make Sugar Cookie Sword: In the bowl of a stand mixer fitted with paddle attachment, add butter and sugar and cream on medium speed 1 minute. Add in eggs and vanilla and mix 1 minute. Sprinkle in flour, baking powder, baking soda, and salt and mix until well combined. Form into a round disk, wrap in plastic wrap, and refrigerate 1 hour.
4. Preheat oven to 400°F. Line a baking sheet with parchment paper.

(continued) ▶

For Pudding

- 1 (3.4-ounce) box instant vanilla pudding
- 1½ cups whole milk
- 12 chocolate sandwich cookies
- 1 (8-ounce) tub frozen whipped topping, thawed

5. Roll out dough on a lightly floured surface to ¼" thickness. Use a 3"–4" sword cookie cutter to cut out four little swords (feel free to make extra with dough). Place cut dough onto prepared baking sheet and bake 6–8 minutes until bottoms are browned and tops are no longer soft. Remove from oven and allow to cool completely on baking sheet, about 1 hour.
6. To make Pudding: Mix vanilla pudding powder with milk in a medium bowl and allow to sit 5 minutes to set.
7. Blend sandwich cookies in a blender or food processor. Fold into Pudding along with whipped topping.
8. To assemble, scoop Pudding into four cups. Place 1 Sugar Cookie Sword into the middle of each cup and sprinkle Streusel Topping around each sword. Serve immediately.

Johnny Appleseed's Warm Apple Cakes

····· **The Diamond Horseshoe, Magic Kingdom** ·····

These individual little cakes are as adorable as they are scrumptious. Johnny Appleseed is an American legend who planted apple trees everywhere he went and ended up fruiting much of America with delicious apples. Johnny was actually a real person named John Chapman and really did plant an abundance of apple trees! Enjoy this dessert as you wonder whether Johnny himself planted the tree that these apples came from.

YIELDS 10 CAKES

- 1½ cups salted butter, melted
- 1½ cups granulated sugar
- ½ cup light brown sugar
- 1 teaspoon baking soda
- 1 teaspoon ground cinnamon
- ½ teaspoon ground nutmeg
- ½ teaspoon salt
- 2 teaspoons vanilla extract
- 3 cups all-purpose flour, divided
- 3 large eggs
- 3 medium Gala apples, peeled, cored, and finely diced
- 10 tablespoons whipped salted butter
- ½ cup caramel topping

1. Preheat oven to 325°F. Spray two jumbo-muffin tins with nonstick cooking spray.
2. In the bowl of a stand mixer fitted with paddle attachment, cream together butter and sugars on medium speed until well combined, about 2 minutes. Sprinkle in baking soda, cinnamon, nutmeg, salt, and vanilla while continuing to mix. Add in 1½ cups flour and mix 1 minute. Add in eggs one at a time and mix 30 seconds between additions. Add remaining 1½ cups flour and mix 1 minute more. Add in apples and mix until just incorporated.
3. Scoop batter into muffin divots, filling each divot about ½–¾ full. Bake 30–40 minutes until a knife inserted in the center comes out clean. Allow to cool in pan about 5 minutes.
4. Place cakes on individual plates and top each with 1 tablespoon whipped butter. Drizzle caramel topping over cakes. Serve warm.

Vegan Blackberry Cupcakes

····• Sunshine Seasons, EPCOT •····

It's hard to believe these cupcakes have no real butter in them! They are so fluffy and creamy that it is impossible to tell. Sunshine Seasons is in The Land pavilion at EPCOT, which also houses the Soarin' Around the World and Living with the Land attractions. Grabbing a bite here is the perfect break between riding those two attractions (anything to stay in the AC a little longer!).

YIELDS 12 CUPCAKES

For Vegan Vanilla Cupcakes

1¾ cups all-purpose flour
1 cup granulated sugar
1 teaspoon baking soda
½ teaspoon salt
1 cup soy milk
2 teaspoons vanilla extract
⅓ cup plant-based buttery spread, melted
1 tablespoon apple cider vinegar

For Vegan "Buttercream" Frosting

3½ cups confectioners' sugar
1 cup plant-based butter
¼ teaspoon salt

1. To make Vegan Vanilla Cupcakes: Preheat oven to 350°F. Line a cupcake tin with cupcake papers.
2. Add flour, sugar, baking soda, and salt to a large bowl. Stir to combine. Add in soy milk, vanilla, melted spread, and apple cider vinegar. Stir until there are no floury chunks. Divide batter evenly among the cupcake liners so that each liner is about ¾ full. Bake 15–18 minutes until a knife inserted in the center comes out clean. Remove from oven and allow to cool completely in the tin, about 1 hour.
3. To make Vegan "Buttercream" Frosting: In a medium bowl, add all ingredients and stir just until combined and smooth.

2 teaspoons vanilla extract

3 drops purple gel food coloring

For Assembly

12 tablespoons blackberry jam

½ cup Mickey sprinkles

12 whole blackberries

4. **To Assemble:** Use a tablespoon to scoop out the center of each cupcake. Fill each with 1 tablespoon blackberry jam. Scoop 1–2 tablespoons Vegan "Buttercream" Frosting onto each cupcake. Press Mickey sprinkles around the edges of the frosting and place a blackberry on top in the center of frosting. Serve immediately.

Serving Suggestion

These come with a lot of frosting at Disney. If you aren't partial to the 50 percent frosting to 50 percent cake ratio, go ahead and spread less frosting on. On the other hand, if you want twice as much frosting, just double the frosting recipe.

Berry Short Cake

······ **Garden Grill Restaurant, EPCOT** ······

Berry Short Cake is *the* dessert to top off your family-style meal at Garden Grill Restaurant. This rotating restaurant in The Land pavilion at EPCOT gives diners a bird's-eye peek at the Living with the Land attraction. You may even get visits from characters like Chip and Dale, Pluto, and the big mouse himself: Mickey! Dinner includes unlimited portions of such fare as salad, mashed potatoes, grilled beef, and macaroni and cheese. If you don't save room while at Garden Grill for the Berry Short Cake, don't worry! You can make it at home when you aren't so full.

SERVES 2

½ cup salted butter, softened
½ cup granulated sugar
2 large eggs
1 teaspoon vanilla extract
¼ teaspoon salt
1 cup all-purpose flour
1 cup mixed berries
1 tablespoon pure maple syrup
1 tablespoon lemon juice
2 tablespoons whipped cream

1. Preheat oven to 350°F. Coat a mini loaf pan in baking flour spray.
2. In the bowl of a stand mixer fitted with paddle attachment, cream butter and sugar together on medium speed 1 minute. Add in eggs, vanilla, and salt and mix 1 minute. Add in flour and mix until just combined.
3. Scoop batter into prepared loaf pan and bake 45–55 minutes until a knife inserted in the center comes out clean. Remove from oven and allow to cool in pan 10 minutes.
4. In a small saucepan, add berries, maple syrup, and lemon juice. Bring to a boil over medium-high heat, pressing with a potato masher to release juices. Reduce heat to low and cook 3–4 minutes or when slightly thickened. Remove from heat and allow to cool 10 minutes.
5. To serve, cut cake into two slices and top each slice with a scoop of berries and 1 tablespoon whipped cream.

Grapefruit Cake

The Hollywood Brown Derby, Disney's Hollywood Studios

This cake has just the right tart-to-sweet ratio and will be loved even by those who aren't typically fans of grapefruit. The white chocolate decoration on top elevates this cake from a simpler treat to a decadent dessert befitting the finest Hollywood elite. The walls of The Hollywood Brown Derby where this recipe is served are dotted with caricature portraits of the Hollywood elite across the last century. Have you found any of your favorite movie stars?

SERVES 8

For Grapefruit Syrup
- 2 large grapefruits, peeled and sliced
- 1 cup granulated sugar

For Decoration
- ½ cup white chocolate chips
- 2 drops orange gel food coloring

For Cake
- ¾ cup salted butter, softened
- 1 cup granulated sugar
- 3 large eggs
- 1 teaspoon vanilla bean paste
- ¼ cup whole milk
- 1¼ cups self-rising flour
- ½ teaspoon baking powder
- 3 (16-ounce) tubs cream cheese frosting

1. To make Grapefruit Syrup: In a small saucepan over medium heat, add grapefruit slices and sugar. Stir until juices begin to release, then mash with a potato masher until mixture comes to a boil. Remove from heat and pour through a fine-mesh strainer. Refrigerate 1 hour up to overnight.
2. To make Decoration: Place white chocolate chips in a small microwave-safe bowl. Microwave on high 30 seconds, stir, then microwave 30 seconds more and stir. Repeat until chips just melt. Scoop ⅓ chocolate into a separate medium bowl and color with orange food coloring. Lay a sheet of parchment paper on a baking sheet and use a spoon to make 8 butterfly wing shapes out of white chocolate. Use a clean spoon to swipe orange stripes onto wings. Place in freezer until ready to use.
3. To make Cake: Preheat oven to 375°F. Grease two (8") cake pans with nonstick cooking spray and line the bottom of each pan with parchment paper.

(continued) ▶

4. In the bowl of a stand mixer fitted with paddle attachment, add in butter, sugar, eggs, vanilla bean paste, and milk. Mix on medium speed until well combined. Add in flour and baking powder and mix until incorporated and uniform, about 2 minutes. Divide batter between pans and bake 20–30 minutes until a knife inserted in the center comes out clean. Remove from oven and allow to cool completely in pans, about 45 minutes.
5. Remove Cake from pans and slice each cake in half horizontally. Lay one round on a plate. Drizzle with ¼ cup Grapefruit Syrup. Spread ¼ of the cream cheese frosting onto layer. Repeat with remaining Cake rounds. Refrigerate remaining Grapefruit Syrup.
6. Cover entire Cake in a thin layer of cream cheese frosting (as a crumb coat) and refrigerate 30 minutes.
7. Remove Cake from refrigerator and apply a final coat of frosting to sides and top. Use a piece of string to mark 8 equal slices of Cake and top each slice with a white chocolate wing. Keep refrigerated until ready to serve.
8. To serve, cut Cake on pre-marked lines. Drizzle each slice with 1–2 tablespoons Grapefruit Syrup and enjoy.

Wookiee Cookies

Backlot Express, Disney's Hollywood Studios

You don't have to be Maz Kanata to like this Wookiee...Cookie that is! While most Star Wars–themed foods are found in Galaxy's Edge at Disneyland or Disney's Hollywood Studios, this treat is served at Backlot Express, which is next to Star Tours in a separate section of Disney's Hollywood Studios. Two oatmeal cookies sandwich creamy vanilla frosting and are topped with a chocolate decoration reminiscent of the sash Chewbacca wears.

YIELDS 5 COOKIES

For Oatmeal Cookies
- ½ cup salted butter, softened
- ½ cup granulated sugar
- ½ cup light brown sugar
- 1 large egg
- 1 teaspoon vanilla extract
- 1 cup all-purpose flour
- 1 teaspoon ground cinnamon
- ½ teaspoon baking soda
- ½ teaspoon salt
- 1½ cups quick oats

For Vanilla Cream Filling
- 2½ cups confectioners' sugar
- ½ cup vegetable shortening
- ½ teaspoon salt
- 2 teaspoons vanilla bean paste
- 2 teaspoons whole milk

1. To make Oatmeal Cookies: Preheat oven to 375°F. Line a half baking sheet with parchment paper.
2. In the bowl of a stand mixer fitted with paddle attachment, cream butter and sugars on medium speed until well combined, about 1 minute. Add in egg and vanilla and mix 1 minute to combine. Add in flour, cinnamon, baking soda, and salt and mix 2 minutes or until well combined. Fold in oats until incorporated.
3. Use a medium (2-tablespoon) cookie scoop to scoop ten equal-sized mounds of cookie dough and place on prepared baking sheet. Use a greased spatula to gently press down the cookie dough until slightly flat. Bake 10–12 minutes until cookies are browned and cooked through. Allow to cool completely on sheet, about 30 minutes.
4. To make Vanilla Cream Filling: In the bowl of a stand mixer fitted with paddle attachment, add sugar, shortening, salt, and vanilla paste. The mixture will be dry and clumpy. Add in milk until mixture is just creamy and spreadable. Add more milk 1 teaspoon at a time if needed. Set aside.

(continued) ▶

For Milk Chocolate Sashes

½ cup milk chocolate chips

1 teaspoon silver luster dust

5. To make Milk Chocolate Sashes: Place milk chocolate chips in a small microwave-safe bowl and microwave on high 30 seconds. Stir, then microwave 30 seconds more. Stir and repeat until chips just melt. Line a half baking sheet with parchment paper and pour melted chocolate onto parchment. Use an offset spatula or knife to smooth chocolate into a level single layer about ⅙" thick. Freeze solid, about 30 minutes.

6. Remove chocolate from freezer and use a sharp knife to cut chocolate into strips that are each 5½" wide by 4" long (eat or discard excess chocolate). Use luster dust to make a pattern that mimics Chewbacca's sash on each chocolate strip.

7. Place 1 Oatmeal Cookie (flat side up) on a plate and add 2 tablespoons Vanilla Cream Filling, then place another Oatmeal Cookie (flat side down) on top of Vanilla Cream Filling. Spread a small amount of Vanilla Cream Filling on the back of 1 Milk Chocolate Sash and place on top of cookie. Repeat to make 5 cookies (cookies can be stored in the refrigerator up to 3 days).

Cooking Hack

These cookies are just as delicious without the chocolate sash, so if you're looking to get them on the table quicker, go ahead and omit it.

Fried Wontons

Yak & Yeti Restaurant, Disney's Animal Kingdom

Fried Wontons may sound like a savory dish, but the Yak & Yeti Restaurant makes them sweet. Each wonton wrapper holds sweet cream cheese and is deep-fried to perfection. But what really makes this dish is the fresh pineapple chunks and honey-vanilla drizzle. If you'd rather use the drizzle as a dip, have at it! Yak & Yeti Restaurant has an eclectic collection of Nepalese decor, each room containing fascinating artwork, like portraits, statuettes, and brass altar pieces.

SERVES 2

- 48 ounces vegetable oil, for frying
- ¼ cup whipped cream cheese
- 1 tablespoon confectioners' sugar
- 8 square wonton wrappers
- 1 cup vanilla Greek yogurt
- 2 tablespoons honey
- ½ teaspoon vanilla extract
- 8 chunks fresh pineapple
- ½ cup sliced fresh strawberries
- 2 (¼-cup) scoops vanilla ice cream
- 2 fresh mint leaves

1. Pour oil in a large shallow pot or deep fryer and preheat to 350°F. Line a plate with paper towels.
2. In a small bowl, mix cream cheese and confectioners' sugar. Lay out 1 wonton wrapper and run a moistened finger around the edges of wrapper. Scoop about 1 teaspoon cream cheese mixture into the center of wonton wrapper. Roll up like a burrito and then pinch the two ends together. Make sure all filling is pinched inside the wrapper. Repeat with remaining wrappers.
3. Carefully drop wontons into preheated oil. Fry 2–4 minutes, turning frequently, until wontons are golden brown. Transfer to prepared plate to drain.
4. In a small bowl, mix yogurt, honey, and vanilla.
5. Take one skewer and add pieces in this order: wonton, pineapple chunk, pineapple chunk, wonton. Repeat with remaining skewers. Lay two skewers each on two serving plates in an X pattern. Sprinkle each plate with ¼ cup sliced strawberries and top with honey-vanilla drizzle. Place a scoop of ice cream onto each of two serving plates and top with mint leaves. Serve immediately.

Chocolate Cake

Satu'li Canteen, Disney's Animal Kingdom

Originally called Neytiri's Chocolate Cake, named after the fierce warrior of the Na'vi (and one of the main characters of the Avatar films), this dessert is hardly recognizable as a chocolate cake at all. Shaped like one large dome with a small dome on top, Pandoran chocolate cake is very unlike chocolate cakes found on Earth. But the flavors are similar to those in a chocolate mousse, with silky and creamy chocolate wrapped around a crunchy cookie center. The chocolate circle decoration and goji berries add to the planetary look.

SERVES 8

For Chocolate Cake Base
- 8 speculoos cookies, crushed
- ½ cup chocolate-hazelnut spread
- 3 tablespoons salted butter
- 1 cup semisweet chocolate chips
- 3 large eggs, yolks and whites separated
- ½ teaspoon cream of tartar
- ¼ cup plus 2 tablespoons granulated sugar, divided
- ½ cup heavy whipping cream
- ½ teaspoon vanilla extract
- 1 tablespoon cocoa powder

1. To make Chocolate Cake Base: In a small bowl, mix cookies and chocolate-hazelnut spread. Fill eight (1.5") divots of a semicircle silicone mold with mixture. Place in freezer to set 1 hour.
2. In a medium microwave-safe bowl, microwave butter and chocolate chips 30 seconds, stir, then microwave 30 seconds more and stir until melted and smooth. Let cool 10 minutes, then stir in egg yolks. Set aside.
3. In the bowl of a stand mixer fitted with whisk attachment, beat egg whites on medium-high speed 2 minutes. Add cream of tartar and beat until soft peaks form, 2–4 minutes. Add in ¼ cup sugar and continue beating until stiff peaks form, 2–4 more minutes. Fold mixture carefully into chocolate and yolk mixture. Clean out mixer bowl.
4. In mixer bowl, beat heavy cream on medium-high speed 2 minutes. Add remaining 2 tablespoons sugar and vanilla and continue to beat 2–4 minutes more until stiff peaks form. Fold into chocolate mixture.

For Banana Cream Topping

1 large ripe banana, peeled
2 teaspoons honey
1/8 teaspoon lemon juice
4 tablespoons heavy whipping cream
1 tablespoon confectioners' sugar

For Assembly

1/4 cup semisweet chocolate chips
1 teaspoon coconut oil
1 teaspoon gold luster dust
8 dried goji berries
16 tablespoons diced fresh pineapple

5. Dust eight (3") divots of a separate semicircle silicone mold with cocoa powder and scoop in chocolate mixture, filling 3/4 full. Remove cookie circles from first mold and press into the center of each chocolate divot. Refrigerate 3 hours to set.

6. To make Banana Cream Topping: Add bananas, honey, and lemon juice to a blender. Blend until smooth. Add heavy whipping cream and pulse 1 minute to combine.

7. Dust eight (1") divots of a third semicircle silicone mold with confectioners' sugar. Scoop Banana Cream Topping into mold (eat or discard leftovers) and refrigerate 1 hour to set.

8. To Assemble: Make chocolate decoration by adding semisweet chocolate chips and coconut oil to a medium microwave-safe bowl. Microwave 30 seconds, stir, and microwave 30 seconds more, then stir and repeat until chocolate just melts. Spread chocolate in a thin (1/16") layer on a sheet of parchment paper and freeze 1 hour to set. Use a 2" circular cookie cutter to cut eight circles out of chocolate.

9. Place 1 Chocolate Cake Base in a shallow bowl. Sprinkle with gold luster dust. Unmold 1 Banana Cream Topping and place on top of Chocolate Cake Base. Drive 1 chocolate circle into the top of the Chocolate Cake Base and place 1 goji berry on top of Banana Cream Topping. Sprinkle 2 tablespoons pineapple bits around the bowl. Repeat with remaining ingredients to make eight servings and serve immediately.

Honey Bee Cupcakes

••••• **Restaurantosaurus, Disney's Animal Kingdom** •••••

Packed with honey flavors and honey decorations, these cupcakes will have everyone buzzing to get their hands on one. Restaurantosaurus is a Quick Service restaurant found in DinoLand U.S.A. at Disney's Animal Kingdom. Did you know that there is a restaurant "backstage" behind Restaurantosaurus called Castasaurus? This behind-the-scenes eatery serves hot meals to Cast Members who work at Disney's Animal Kingdom.

YIELDS 24 CUPCAKES

For Cupcakes
- 1 (16.25-ounce) box white cake mix
- 1 cup pulp-free orange juice
- ½ cup vegetable oil
- 3 large eggs

For Honey Bavarian Filling
- 1 (3.4-ounce) box instant vanilla pudding
- 1½ cups heavy whipping cream
- 1 tablespoon honey

For Honey Buttercream Frosting
- 1 cup salted butter, softened
- 4 cups confectioners' sugar
- ¼ cup honey
- 3 drops yellow gel food coloring
- 3–6 tablespoons whole milk

1. To make Cupcakes: Preheat oven to 350°F. Add black paper cupcake liners to two (twelve-divot) muffin tins and set aside.
2. In a large bowl, whisk together cake mix, orange juice, vegetable oil, and eggs. Divide evenly among prepared muffin cups and bake 14–19 minutes until a knife inserted in the center comes out clean. Remove from oven and allow to cool completely in muffin tins, 30–45 minutes.
3. To make Honey Bavarian Filling: Whisk together instant pudding mix, heavy cream, and honey until light and fluffy. Scoop into a piping bag with a medium circular tip and set aside.
4. To make Honey Buttercream Frosting: In the bowl of a stand mixer fitted with whisk attachment, mix butter, confectioners' sugar, honey, and yellow food coloring on medium speed. Add in milk 1 tablespoon at a time until consistency is fluffy but tight. Scoop into a piping bag with a medium circular tip and set aside.

(continued) ▶

For White Chocolate Honeycomb

1 cup white chocolate chips

1 tablespoon gold luster dust

For Assembly

24 honeybee sugar decorations

½ cup yellow and black crunchy pearls

5. To make White Chocolate Honeycomb: Place white chocolate chips in a medium microwave-safe bowl and microwave 30 seconds, stir, and microwave 30 seconds more and stir again. Repeat until chocolate just melts. Lay out a 2' square piece of clean standard Bubble Wrap. Use an offset spatula or knife to smooth melted chocolate in a single, thin layer over Bubble Wrap and freeze 15 minutes to set. Remove from freezer and use a sharp knife to cut chocolate into 1" triangles. Brush gold luster dust onto just the top of the bubbled side of each triangle. Set aside.

6. To Assemble: Scoop 1 tablespoon of cake out of the center of each Cupcake. Eat or discard cake pieces. Swirl Honey Bavarian Filling into each cupcake divot, then swirl Honey Buttercream Frosting over entire Cupcake surface. Lay 1 White Chocolate Honeycomb triangle on each Cupcake and place 1 honeybee sugar decoration next to it. Sprinkle each Cupcake with crunchy pearls and serve immediately or refrigerate until ready to serve. Extras can be kept sealed in the refrigerator up to 1 week.

Strawberry Shortcake Funnel Cake Fries

...... Award Wieners, Disney California Adventure ......

And the award for yummiest and most easily sharable dessert goes to...Strawberry Shortcake Funnel Cake Fries! This summer sensation at the Park can be enjoyed any time of year when you make them at home. Award Wieners changes its Funnel Cake Fries throughout the year with different in-season fruits. You can do the same! Grab whatever is popular at your local farmers' market to top these fries.

SERVES 1

- 48 ounces vegetable oil, for frying
- 2 large eggs
- 1 tablespoon water
- ¼ cup granulated sugar
- ½ cup whole milk
- 2 teaspoons vanilla extract
- 2 cups all-purpose flour
- 1 teaspoon baking powder
- ½ teaspoon salt
- 2 tablespoons cinnamon sugar
- 1 cup canned whipped cream
- 2 tablespoons strawberry syrup
- 1 fresh whole strawberry, hulled
- 3 leaves fresh mint, cut into strips

1. Pour oil into a large shallow pot or deep fryer and heat to 350°F. Line a half baking sheet with parchment paper. Line a plate with paper towels.
2. In a medium bowl, whisk together eggs, water, sugar, milk, and vanilla. Add in flour, baking powder, and salt and stir with a spoon until combined.
3. Scoop into a piping bag with a ¼" piping tip or opening at the end of the bag. Pipe in long strips across parchment paper; continue on a second sheet if necessary. Place sheet(s) into freezer and chill 30 minutes or until strips can be lifted off the parchment paper without breaking or sticking.
4. Working with 1 strip of dough at a time, pull strip off the parchment paper, then use kitchen scissors to snip into 4" strips. Carefully drop each strip into oil and allow to fry about 5 minutes, turning frequently, or until golden brown. Transfer to a prepared plate and allow oil to drain.

(continued) ▶

5. Toss fries in cinnamon sugar, then pile fries onto a large plate. Spray whipped cream in a swirl on the center of fries. Drizzle with strawberry syrup and add whole strawberry to side of whipped cream pile. Sprinkle with mint strips and serve immediately.

Disney Parks Tip

Award Wieners is right across from the Animation Academy, a fun place at Disney California Adventure where you can learn to sketch some of your favorite Disney characters.

Celestial-Sized Candy Bar: Choco-Smash CANDY Bar

······· **Pym Test Kitchen, Disney California Adventure** ·······

These have been termed the "best thing in the Park" by popular Instagrammers @WeKnowDisney; now you can be the judge. Packed full of all the best things a chocolate bar can offer—and then some—each bite is exciting. Hank Pym truly outdid himself when he decided to make this bar "celestial-sized." With a recipe that serves eight, you can share the goodness with your friends and family!

SERVES 8

- 1 tablespoon salted butter
- 2 cups white chocolate chips
- 2 cups mini marshmallows
- 12 ounces prepared milk chocolate brownies
- 4 (2.22-ounce) bags Werther's soft caramels, unwrapped
- 4 tablespoons whole milk
- ½ cup dry roasted unsalted peanuts
- 1 cup creamy peanut butter
- ½ cup confectioners' sugar
- 2 (12-ounce) bags dark chocolate chips

1. Grease a deep chocolate bar mold with nonstick cooking spray and set aside. Line an 8" × 8" baking dish with parchment paper.
2. In a large microwave-safe bowl, add butter, white chocolate chips, and mini marshmallows. Microwave and stir in 30-second increments until completely melted and combined. Pour into prepared baking dish and refrigerate about 1 hour or until solid.
3. Cut brownies to fit snugly into bottom of candy bar mold to just cover bottom ¼".
4. In a large microwave-safe bowl, add caramels and milk. Microwave and stir in 30-second increments until completely melted and combined. Stir in peanuts and scoop and spread on top of brownies in thin layer.
5. Remove nougat from refrigerator. Cut to fit into candy bar mold on top of caramel. Eat or discard any excess.
6. Mix together peanut butter and confectioners' sugar in a small bowl and scoop into a piping bag with a medium round tip. Squirt in a line in a scallop pattern across top of nougat. If candy bar mold is wide, make a second line of peanut butter across top. Place candy bar mold in refrigerator 1 hour to set.

7. Line a baking sheet with parchment paper and set aside. In a large microwave-safe bowl, add semisweet chocolate chips. Microwave and stir in 30-second increments until completely melted. Remove candy from mold (and cut in half lengthwise if you used a wide mold). Carefully lower each candy bar into chocolate with a fork and completely coat in chocolate. Allow excess chocolate to drip off, then place onto prepared baking sheet. Allow to set at room temperature 1 hour, then serve. Store candy bars in a sealed container at room temperature up to 1 week.

Serving Suggestion

To have a more authentic experience, look up a printable for the wrapper of this candy bar. Print it out and cover it in clear packing tape to protect against the chocolate. Your friends will not be able to tell the difference between the ones served at Disney and the ones you make!

Hazelnut Crunch Mickey Pops

••••• **Carthay Circle Restaurant, Disney California Adventure** •••••

This delicious little ice cream treat can be enjoyed at both Carthay Circle Restaurant and Carthay Circle Lounge. The former is on the top floor of the Carthay Circle building near the front of Disney California Adventure Park. The lounge is in the same building but occupies the cushy chairs and tables on the ground floor. They have different menus, but everything is fresh and tasty. If you want to get ambitious, make your own vanilla bean ice cream to use in these pops!

SERVES 2

- 2 rounded scoops vanilla bean ice cream
- 1 (3.1-ounce) bar hazelnut milk chocolate, broken into pieces
- ⅓ cup white chocolate chips
- 4 milk chocolate candy melt circles

1. Line a plate with parchment paper. Place ice cream on parchment and drive a Popsicle stick into the top of each scoop. Put in freezer to set 30 minutes.
2. In a medium microwave-safe bowl, add hazelnut chocolate bar and white chocolate chips. Microwave 30 seconds, stir, then microwave 30 seconds more and stir again. Repeat until chocolate just melts.
3. Remove ice cream from freezer and carefully spoon melted chocolate over ice cream until completely coated. Top with 2 chocolate candy melts each on either side of Popsicle sticks to resemble Mickey ears. Return to freezer 30 minutes more, then serve.

CHAPTER 8

Drinks

This last chapter is full of all your favorite Disney beverages, from Galaxy's Edge sips the whole family can enjoy, like Meiloorun Juice, to the adult libations of EPCOT, like the Black Magic. Drinks are a quick and easy way to bring a bit of Disney magic into your home with few ingredients and no special bartending skills needed.

    Each alcoholic recipe up ahead also includes notes for making the drink without alcohol. So unlike at Disney, kids at home can grab a mocktail version of the Yub Nub or Violet Silk Martini and give it a try. And don't be afraid to make these drinks yours! Swap out flavors to use your favorites, serve the drinks in your funkiest glasses, and try out creative garnishes. Here, you're the bartender, and whatever you make will be infused with Disney magic.

Cold Brew Black Caf

Docking Bay 7 Food and Cargo, Disneyland and Disney's Hollywood Studios

Mere Earthlings couldn't have come up with this idea: chocolate puff cereal in a coffee! But all the humans are clamoring to get their hands on it. Debuting at Galaxy's Edge West at Disneyland in California, it became so popular that it flew across the country to Galaxy's Edge East and is now also served at Disney's Hollywood Studios in Florida. The whipped cream cheese provides a creamy note that complements the strong cold brew coffee. If you don't drink coffee, replace the cold brew with a coffee substitute.

SERVES 1

- ¼ cup whipped cream cheese
- 2 tablespoons half-and-half
- ½ tablespoon granulated sugar
- 1 cup cold brew coffee
- 1 cup crushed ice
- ¼ cup whole chocolate puff cereal

1. In a blender, add whipped cream cheese, half-and-half, and sugar. Blend until well combined and frothy, about 2 minutes.
2. Pour cold brew coffee into a plastic cup or glass and add ice. Pour in frothy topping and sprinkle with cereal. Serve immediately.

Yub Nub

••••••• **Oga's Cantina at Disneyland and Disney's Hollywood Studios** •••••••

"Yub Nub" was the celebratory song sung by the Ewoks at the end of Star Wars: Episode 6, *Return of the Jedi*, and this drink was crafted in reference to that song. In fact, if you order this drink at Oga's Cantina, it comes in a tiki tumbler that depicts the towering pine trees of Endor and retreating Imperial sky ships. You can purchase the tumbler to make the Yub Nub at home in the official cup!

SERVES 1

2 ounces passion fruit juice
1½ ounces simple syrup
1 ounce pineapple rum
1 ounce spiced rum
¼ ounce lemon juice
¼ ounce lime juice

1. Add all ingredients to a cocktail shaker filled with ice and shake.
2. Strain into a tiki glass filled with crushed ice.

Make It a Mocktail!

To make a tasty mocktail for the whole family to enjoy, simply add 2 ounces passion fruit juice, 1½ ounces cinnamon syrup, 1 ounce pineapple juice, ¼ ounce lemon juice, and ¼ ounce lime juice to a cocktail shaker filled with ice. Shake, then strain over crushed ice into a tiki glass.

Meiloorun Juice

Ronto Roasters, Disneyland

A meiloorun is a fictional fruit found in the Star Wars universe that apparently has notes of pineapple, lemon, blueberry, cranberry, and desert pear. This fruit has featured prominently in several episodes of the animated series *Star Wars Rebels*, including one episode where Ezra was sent on a fool's errand by Kanaan to find some meiloorun. Although it truly would be a fool's errand to try and find a meiloorun at your local grocery store, this recipe mimics the flavors.

SERVES 1

- 2 ounces pineapple juice
- 6 ounces lemonade with blueberry
- 2 ounces cranberry juice
- ½ ounce lemon juice
- ½ ounce Monin Desert Pear Syrup

Add all ingredients to a cocktail shaker with 1 cup ice. Shake until well combined and pour into a plastic cup or glass. Top off with ice cubes to fill and serve.

Hurricane Cocktail

••••• **Blue Bayou Restaurant, Disneyland** •••••

There are a few things iconic to New Orleans: beignets, voodoo, jazz music, and hurricanes. Hurricanes seem to rock New Orleans like clockwork, and citizens of NOLA know how to batten down the hatches and take the storms in stride—such stride, actually, that they named a cocktail after them! This tasty concoction found at Blue Bayou Restaurant won't have you running for the hills; it will have you asking for another. Blue Bayou Restaurant is located *in* the Pirates of the Caribbean attraction at Disneyland and gives a unique dining experience like no other.

SERVES 1

- 1 ounce Bacardí Reserva Ocho rum
- 1 ounce dark rum of choice
- 1 ounce passion fruit purée
- 1 ounce pulp-free orange juice
- ¾ ounce grenadine
- ½ ounce lime juice
- ½ ounce simple syrup
- 1 orange wheel, scored
- 1 maraschino cherry

1. Add all ingredients except orange wheel and cherry to a cocktail shaker filled with ice and shake.
2. Pour into a hurricane glass, then add ice to fill.
3. Garnish with orange wheel on rim and place cherry to float on ice.

Make It a Mocktail!

Swap the rum for an extra ounce each of orange juice and passion fruit purée and follow the directions as usual.

Happy Haunts Milk Shake

Columbia Harbour House, Magic Kingdom

Welcome, foolish mortal, to the Happy Haunts Milk Shake! Have no fear: This milkshake is both a beverage and a snack in one. Sip on the fruity blackberry milkshake and have a bite of the chocolate cake doughnut. It may very well be the perfect combination.

SERVES 1

- 1 cup confectioners' sugar
- ½ teaspoon vanilla extract
- ¼ cup plus 2 tablespoons whole milk, divided
- 2 drops purple gel food coloring
- 1 chocolate glazed doughnut
- 1 tablespoon black stick sprinkles
- 2 ounces Monin Blackberry Purée
- 3 cups vanilla ice cream

1. In a small bowl, combine confectioners' sugar, vanilla extract, 2 tablespoons whole milk, and purple food coloring to make frosting. Dip top surface of doughnut into frosting and place on a wire cooling rack over a baking sheet. Sprinkle frosting with sprinkles and allow frosting to set, about 30 minutes.
2. In a blender, add blackberry purée, ice cream, and remaining ¼ cup whole milk. Blend until well combined. Pour into a plastic cup or glass and insert a large-gauge straw. Slide frosted doughnut over straw and rest on rim. Serve immediately.

Adventureland Colada

Jungle Navigation Co. LTD Skipper Canteen, Magic Kingdom

If your siestas feel like they are getting shorter and shorter, grab your amigos and whip up a batch of Adventureland Coladas. The delectable combo of pineapple, coconut, and passion fruit will have you feeling like you've been transported straight to Walt Disney's Enchanted Tiki Room. For a switch-up, try drizzling different flavors of purée instead of passion fruit. The combinations are endless!

SERVES 1

4 ounces pineapple juice
1 ounce simple syrup
2 ounces cream of coconut
3 cups crushed ice
1 ounce Monin Passion Fruit Purée
1 wedge fresh pineapple

1. In a blender, add pineapple juice, simple syrup, cream of coconut, and ice. Blend until smooth.
2. Drizzle purée around the inside of a plastic cup or glass. Pour blended drink into prepared cup and top with pineapple wedge. Serve immediately.

Lightyear Lemonade

Space 220 Restaurant, EPCOT

Named after our favorite Space Ranger—Buzz Lightyear—this drink will take you to infinity and beyond. In fact, dining at Space 220 Restaurant at EPCOT does just that, as diners are taken in a "space elevator" seemingly 220 miles above Earth's surface. Your house might not have a space elevator (yet) but drinking this lemonade will take you someplace cool for sure!

SERVES 1

1 butterfly pea tea bag
8 ounces cold lemonade
7 fresh mint leaves, divided

1. Pour 8 ounces boiling water into a cup. Add butterfly pea tea bag and allow to steep 5 minutes. Remove tea bag, squeezing out remaining juices, discard bag, and refrigerate tea until cooled, about 1 hour.
2. In a cocktail shaker, add 2 ounces of cooled butterfly pea tea, lemonade, and 6 mint leaves. Muddle leaves, add 1 cup ice, and shake to combine.
3. Pour into a plastic cup or glass and discard muddled leaves. Top with ice and garnish with remaining mint leaf. Serve.

Black Magic

La Hacienda de San Angel, EPCOT

Unlike every other recipe in this book, this drink was not created by Disney chefs, but by a celebrity! That's right—actor Neil Patrick Harris actually invented this drink specifically for the Mexico pavilion at EPCOT. An outspoken fan of Disney, Neil Patrick Harris not only mixes drinks, but also can be seen almost every year presenting at the EPCOT International Festival of the Holidays—Candlelight Processional.

SERVES 1

½ cup ice cubes
2 ounces blackberry purée
1½ ounces mezcal
¾ ounce simple syrup
½ ounce black currant liqueur (also called cassis)
½ ounce lime juice
1 fresh mint leaf

1. Add all ingredients except mint leaf to a blender and blend until smooth.
2. Serve in a martini glass with floating mint leaf on top.

Make It a Mocktail!

Simply swap the mezcal and black currant liqueur for 2 ounces water and follow recipe instructions.

Violet Silk Martini

• • • • Tokyo Dining, EPCOT • • • •

Violet Silk Martini is a fan favorite at EPCOT and consistently makes the "best" lists for "drinking around the world." If you haven't heard of "drinking around the world," it's where guests challenge themselves to drink one alcoholic beverage at each of the eleven World Showcase countries of EPCOT. If you've always wanted to try the Violet Silk Martini but don't imbibe in alcohol, check out the recipe note on how to make it alcohol-free!

SERVES 1

1½ ounces vodka
1½ ounces purple pear syrup
½ ounce lime juice
1 lime wheel

1. Add all ingredients except lime wheel to a cocktail shaker filled with ice. Shake and strain into a martini glass.
2. Garnish with floating lime wheel. Serve.

Make It a Mocktail!

Simply sub out the vodka for 1 ½ ounces of water and follow recipe instructions.

Orbiting Oreos

•••••• **Sci-Fi Dine-In Theater Restaurant, Disney's Hollywood Studios** ••••••

A playful riff on the classic Oreo Cookie milkshake, this one is made for adults, with a chocolate liqueur flavoring. Blend up some for a backyard movie night in the summer, with a batch of the mocktail version for the kiddos. To make it even more authentic, find a super cheesy sci-fi movie to watch so you can have that full Sci-Fi Dine-In Theater Restaurant experience.

SERVES 1

½ cup vanilla ice cream
½ cup whole milk
2 ounces chocolate liqueur
4 Oreo cookies, crushed
Whipped cream
1 glow cube

1. Add ice cream, milk, chocolate liqueur, and crushed Oreo cookies to a blender. Blend until smooth.
2. Pour into a highball glass, top with whipped cream, and garnish with glow cube.

Make It a Mocktail!

Just replace the chocolate liqueur with chocolate syrup and follow the recipe instructions!

Mowie Wowie

50's Prime Time Café, Disney's Hollywood Studios

50's Prime Time Café has been made famous by its colorful servers who push customers around, but this drink has its own claim to fame with its fun and fruity flavor profile. You'll be proclaiming "Wowie!" in your own home after mixing up this drink. Make a large batch to share with friends.

SERVES 1

- 2 ounces coconut rum
- ½ ounce melon liqueur
- ½ ounce peach schnapps
- ½ ounce pulp-free orange juice
- ½ ounce pineapple juice
- 1 glow cube

1. Add all ingredients except glow cube to a cocktail shaker filled with ice and shake.
2. Pour into a highball glass, add ice to fill, and garnish with glow cube.

Make It a Mocktail!

Instead of using rum, melon liqueur, and peach schnapps, just use 3 ounces of water! Follow the recipe instructions as usual.

Fichwa Maji

Harambe Market, Disney's Animal Kingdom

Named after the famous "hidden" Mickey on the wall of Harambe, *fichwa* literally means "hidden"! *Maji* means "water," and while this drink looks like water, it is actually a fruity concoction filled with bright flavors. In order to get one of these at the Park, head to the back of the Harambe Market to a little stall that "locals" call HaramBar. Here you can get drinks with or without alcohol.

SERVES 1

- 8 ounces pineapple juice
- 1 ounce blue curaçao
- 1 ounce Monin Coconut Syrup
- 1 slice pineapple with rind on

1. In a cocktail shaker, mix together pineapple juice, blue curaçao, and syrup. Add 1 cup ice and shake until well combined.
2. Pour into a plastic cup or glass, fill to the top with ice, and garnish with pineapple slice on rim. Serve.

Rum Blossoms

••••• **Pongu Pongu, Disney's Animal Kingdom** •••••

The Rum Blossom and its nonalcoholic sister drink, the Night Blossom, are some of the most popular drinks at Disney's Animal Kingdom. And it's no wonder: The frozen fruity flavors with literal pops of juice from the boba balls make for a refreshing drink on a hot Park day. It is also the perfect beverage to make at home for a whole group. Simply place the white rum to the side and guests can add it if they like!

SERVES 2

- 1½ cups limeade
- ½ cup frozen apple juice concentrate
- 4 ounces desert pear syrup
- 1 cup lime sherbet
- ¼ cup lemon-lime soda
- 2 drops green gel food coloring
- 4 ounces white rum
- ½ cup passionfruit boba balls

1. Combine limeade, apple juice concentrate, and desert pear syrup in a pitcher or large mixing bowl. Pour mixture into an ice cream machine and run according to manufacturer's instructions 8 minutes until slushy.
2. In a blender, blend lime sherbet, lemon-lime soda, and green food coloring.
3. Set aside ½ purple limeade mix, and divide remaining ½ between two large plastic cups. Divide green sherbet mix and layer on top of purple limeade in cups, then layer on remaining purple limeade mix. Top each cup with 2 ounces rum, ¼ cup boba balls, and a large-gauge straw.

Make It a Mocktail!

If you omit the white rum from the top, this drink magically becomes the nonalcoholic Night Blossom recipe also sold at Pongu Pongu.

Pingo Doce

••••• **Pym Test Kitchen, Disney California Adventure** •••••

At Pym Test Kitchen, everything is either supersized or shrunk, and the drinks are no exception. You can choose to purchase the Pingo Doce in a *huge* soda can! It is actually a reusable sipper cup, but it looks like a soda can that got enlarged by Pym Particles to be about six times the size of a regular can. The nice thing about souvenir cups is that you can take them home and use them when re-creating drinks in this book. Refill your massive Pingo Doce can with this delicious Pingo Doce recipe!

SERVES 1

8 ounces lemon-lime soda

1½ ounces Monin Vanilla Syrup

In a plastic cup or glass, add lemon-lime soda and vanilla syrup. Stir to combine, top with ice to fill, and serve.

Proton Punch

Pym Test Kitchen, Disney California Adventure

Your little Avengers will definitely assemble when you start making this Proton Punch! Adorned with boba popping pearls and a grenadine-filled pipette, not only is it great for kids to enjoy, but adults will also be reaching for it at your next Marvel viewing party. If you don't have any pipettes, check out Chapter 2 for information on how to get some or what to use as a substitute.

SERVES 1

8 ounces lemonade
1 ounce Monin Wildberry Purée
¼ cup cherry-flavored popping pearls
¼ ounce grenadine

1. In a plastic cup or glass, add lemonade and purée. Stir gently.
2. Fill remainder of cup with ice cubes and carefully scoop popping pearls on top of ice.
3. Fill a plastic pipette with grenadine and place whole pipette into glass. Serve immediately with large-gauge straw. To enjoy, squeeze grenadine from pipette into cup and stir until all ingredients are combined.

Honey Buzz

Pym Tasting Lab, Disney California Adventure

Pym Tasting Lab is a separate bar located next to Pym Test Kitchen and has all kinds of fun drinks and ways to drink them. Beers are placed on a special machine that fills them from the *bottom up*. You can get a flight of miniature IPAs shrunk down and fit onto a ruler. And this drink, the Honey Buzz, is served in a beaker! It is honey-forward in flavor and will have you thinking like The Wasp before the cup is empty.

SERVES 1

For Honey Syrup
½ cup filtered water
½ cup honey

For Cocktail
1½ ounces gin
1 ounce Honey Syrup
¾ ounce lemon juice
1 honey straw

1. To make Honey Syrup: Add water and honey to a small sealable container and stir until well combined.
2. Store in refrigerator up to 2 weeks.
3. To make Cocktail: Add all ingredients except honey straw to a cocktail shaker filled with ice. Shake.
4. Pour into a highball glass and add ice to fill. Garnish with honey straw.

Make It a Mocktail!

Add 2 ounces water, ¾ ounce honey syrup, and ½ ounce lemon juice to a cocktail shaker filled with ice and shake. Pour into a highball glass and add ice to fill. Garnish with a honey straw!

2319

······ **Lamplight Lounge, Disney California Adventure** ······

Named after the famous Pixar desk lamp, Lamplight Lounge pays homage to the great digital animators who brought stories like *Cars*, *Inside Out*, and *Toy Story* to life. This drink derives its name from *Monsters, Inc.* as the emergency code for an escaped child into the monster world. Your little, and not-so-little, monsters alike will enjoy the fruity and tropical flavors of this drink with the added fizz and tang of the Coke on top.

SERVES 1

2 ounces Monin Strawberry Purée
1½ ounces cream of coconut
1½ ounces pineapple juice
3 cups crushed ice
2 ounces Coca-Cola
1 wedge fresh pineapple

1. In a blender, add purée, cream of coconut, pineapple juice, and ice. Blend until smooth and pour into a pint glass.
2. Top with Coca-Cola and garnish with fresh pineapple wedge on glass rim. Serve immediately.

Disney Parks Recipe Locations

Interested in where each of the recipes and restaurants featured in Part 2 are located at the Disney Parks? Use the following maps to find out!

You'll discover a map for each of the six magical locations: Disneyland, Magic Kingdom, EPCOT, Disney's Hollywood Studios, Disney's Animal Kingdom, and Disney California Adventure. Each map includes a numbered key, so you can match a number to a specific recipe, and match the stars next to that number to what restaurant those dishes and/or drinks are found at. Some recipes appear in both Galaxy's Edge locations, while others are unique to one location.

DISNEYLAND

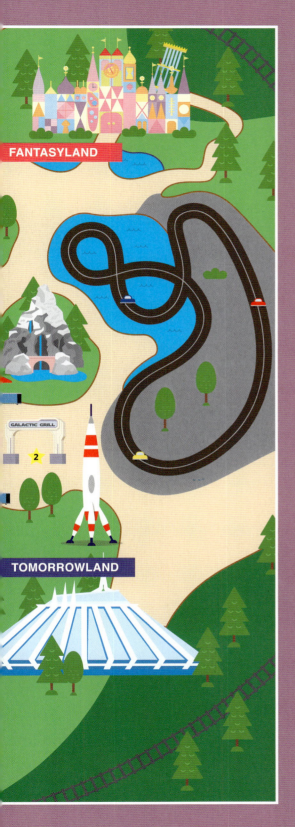

1. **BREAKFAST SANDWICH** (Main Street, U.S.A., Disneyland, Chapter 3: Breakfast)
2. **AMERICAN BREAKFAST BURRITO** (Tomorrowland, Disneyland, Chapter 3: Breakfast)
3. **CINNAMON ROLLS** (Main Street, U.S.A., Disneyland, Chapter 3: Breakfast)
4. **MICKEY-SHAPED PANCAKES** (Fantasyland, Disneyland, Chapter 3: Breakfast)
5. **MUSTAFARIAN LAVA ROLLS** (Star Wars: Galaxy's Edge, Disneyland, Chapter 3: Breakfast)
6. **CHIEFTAIN CHICKEN SKEWERS** (Adventureland, Disneyland, Chapter 4: Lunch)
7. **OUTBACK VEGETABLE SKEWERS** (Adventureland, Disneyland, Chapter 4: Lunch)
8. **RONTO-LESS GARDEN WRAPS** (Star Wars: Galaxy's Edge, Disneyland, Chapter 4: Lunch)
9. **FRIED PICKLES** (Main Street, U.S.A., Disneyland, Chapter 5: Appetizers and Snacks)
10. **FIVE-BLOSSOM BREAD** (Star Wars: Galaxy's Edge, Disneyland, Chapter 5: Appetizers and Snacks)
11. **POMME FRITES** (New Orleans Square, Disneyland, Chapter 5: Appetizers and Snacks)
12. **PLAZA INN SPECIALTY CHICKEN** (Main Street, U.S.A., Disneyland, Chapter 6: Main Dishes)
13. **JAMBALAYA** (New Orleans Square, Disneyland, Chapter 6: Main Dishes)
14. **CRANBERRY ROASTED MEDALLION OF ANGUS BEEF FILET** (New Orleans Square, Disneyland, Chapter 6: Main Dishes)
15. **BATTERED & FRIED MONTE CRISTO** (New Orleans Square, Disneyland, Chapter 6: Main Dishes)
16. **FELUCIAN KEFTA AND HUMMUS GARDEN SPREAD** (Star Wars: Galaxy's Edge, Disneyland, Chapter 6: Main Dishes)
17. **MINE CART BROWNIES** (Main Street, U.S.A., Disneyland, Chapter 7: Desserts)
18. **SWEET LUMPIA!** (Adventureland, Disneyland, Chapter 7: Desserts)
19. **HOUSE-MADE CHOCOLATE-CHUNK COOKIE SUNDAES** (Frontierland, Disneyland, Chapter 7: Desserts)
20. **COLD BREW BLACK CAF** (Star Wars: Galaxy's Edge, Disneyland, Chapter 8: Drinks)
21. **YUB NUB** (Star Wars: Galaxy's Edge, Disneyland, Chapter 8: Drinks)
22. **MEILOORUN JUICE** (Star Wars: Galaxy's Edge, Disneyland, Chapter 8: Drinks)
23. **HURRICANE COCKTAIL** (New Orleans Square, Disneyland, Chapter 8: Drinks)

MAGIC KINGDOM

⭐ 1 **SAUSAGE AND GRAVY TOTS** (Fantasyland, Magic Kingdom, Chapter 3: Breakfast)

⭐ 2 **CINNAMON-SUGAR DOUGHNUTS** (Fantasyland, Magic Kingdom, Chapter 3: Breakfast)

⭐ 3 **DECLARATION SALAD** (Liberty Square, Magic Kingdom, Chapter 4: Lunch)

⭐ 4 **THE SUN BONNET TRIO STRAWBERRY SALAD** (Frontierland, Magic Kingdom, Chapter 4: Lunch)

⭐ 5 **PEANUT BUTTER, CHOCOLATE-HAZELNUT SPREAD, AND BANANA SANDWICH** (Adventureland, Magic Kingdom, Chapter 4: Lunch)

⭐ 6 **FRIED MOZZARELLA** (Main Street, U.S.A., Magic Kingdom, Chapter 5: Appetizers and Snacks)

⭐ 7 **COUNTRY SEASONAL SALAD** (Fantasyland, Magic Kingdom, Chapter 5: Appetizers and Snacks)

⭐ 8 **HOUSE-MADE PEACH APPLESAUCE** (Fantasyland, Magic Kingdom, Chapter 5: Appetizers and Snacks)

⭐ 9 **HERB-SALTED PORK TENDERLOIN** (Fantasyland, Magic Kingdom, Chapter 6: Main Dishes)

⭐ 10 **TENDERLOIN OF BEEF** (Cinderella Castle, Magic Kingdom, Chapter 6: Main Dishes)

⭐ 11 **OOEY GOOEY TOFFEE CAKE** (Liberty Square, Magic Kingdom, Chapter 7: Desserts)

⭐ 12 **THE SWORD IN THE SWEET** (Fantasyland, Magic Kingdom, Chapter 7: Desserts)

⭐ 13 **BUTTERSCOTCH PUDDING** (Main Street, U.S.A., Magic Kingdom, Chapter 7: Desserts)

⭐ 14 **JOHNNY APPLESEED'S WARM APPLE CAKES** (Frontierland, Magic Kingdom, Chapter 7: Desserts)

⭐ 15 **ADVENTURELAND COLADA** (Adventureland, Magic Kingdom, Chapter 8: Drinks)

⭐ 16 **HAPPY HAUNTS MILK SHAKE** (Liberty Square, Magic Kingdom, Chapter 8: Drinks)

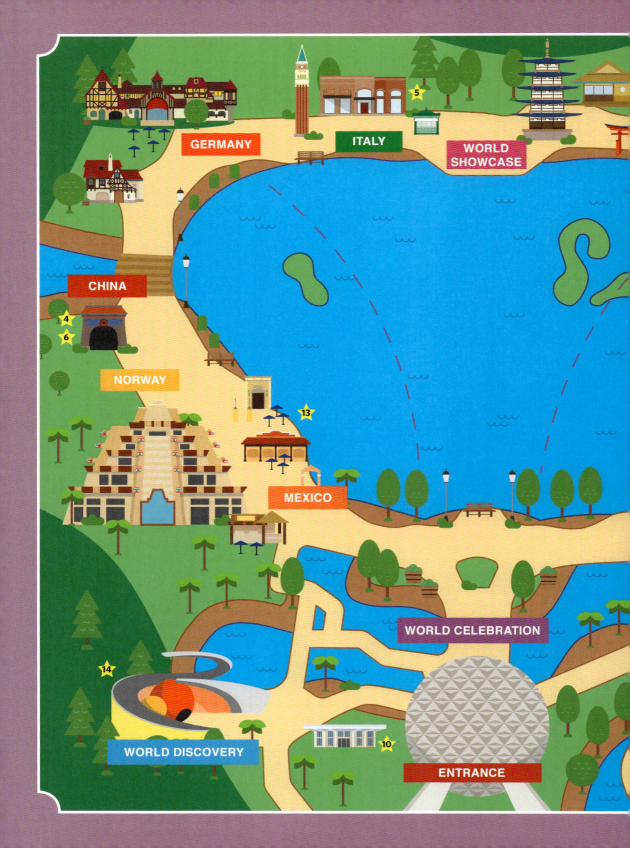

EPCOT

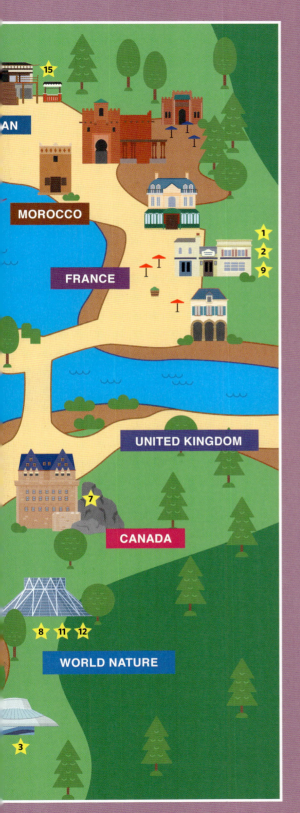

⭐1 **CLASSIQUE GALETTES**
(France Pavilion, EPCOT, Chapter 3: Breakfast)

⭐2 **MELBA CRÊPES**
(France Pavilion, EPCOT, Chapter 3: Breakfast)

⭐3 **LOBSTER BISQUE**
(World Nature, EPCOT, Chapter 4: Lunch)

⭐4 **ORANGE CHICKEN**
(China Pavilion, EPCOT, Chapter 4: Lunch)

⭐5 **CARPACCIO DI MANZO**
(Italy Pavilion, EPCOT, Chapter 5: Appetizers and Snacks)

⭐6 **CHICKEN POT STICKERS**
(China Pavilion, EPCOT, Chapter 5: Appetizers and Snacks)

⭐7 **BABY ICEBERG WEDGE SALAD**
(Canada Pavilion, EPCOT, Chapter 5: Appetizers and Snacks)

⭐8 **VEGETABLE KORMA**
(World Nature, EPCOT, Chapter 6: Main Dishes)

⭐9 **SAVOYARDE GALETTE**
(France Pavilion, EPCOT, Chapter 6: Main Dishes)

⭐10 **CURRY-SPICED PIZZA**
(World Celebration, EPCOT, Chapter 6: Main Dishes)

⭐11 **VEGAN BLACKBERRY CUPCAKES**
(World Nature, EPCOT, Chapter 7: Desserts)

⭐12 **BERRY SHORT CAKE**
(World Nature, EPCOT, Chapter 7: Desserts)

⭐13 **BLACK MAGIC**
(Mexico Pavilion, EPCOT, Chapter 8: Drinks)

⭐14 **LIGHTYEAR LEMONADE**
(World Discovery, EPCOT, Chapter 8: Drinks)

⭐15 **VIOLET SILK MARTINI**
(Japan Pavilion, EPCOT, Chapter 8: Drinks)

DISNEY'S HOLLYWOOD STUDIOS

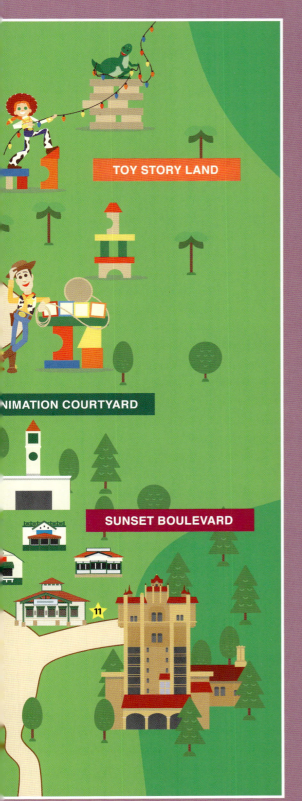

1. **BREAKFAST BOWLS** *(Toy Story Land, Disney's Hollywood Studios, Chapter 3: Breakfast)*
2. **MUSTAFARIAN LAVA ROLLS** *(Star Wars: Galaxy's Edge, Disney's Hollywood Studios, Chapter 3: Breakfast)*
3. **WARM GLAZED DOUGHNUT** *(Commissary Lane, Disney's Hollywood Studios, Chapter 3: Breakfast)*
4. **CARAMEL MONKEY BREAD** *(Echo Lake, Disney's Hollywood Studios, Chapter 3: Breakfast)*
5. **RONTO-LESS GARDEN WRAPS** *(Star Wars: Galaxy's Edge, Disney's Hollywood Studios, Chapter 4: Lunch)*
6. **OUR FAMOUS COBB SALAD** *(Hollywood Boulevard, Disney's Hollywood Studios, Chapter 4: Lunch)*
7. **MARGHERITA FLATBREADS** *(Grand Avenue, Disney's Hollywood Studios, Chapter 4: Lunch)*
8. **"TOTCHOS"** *(Toy Story Land, Disney's Hollywood Studios, Chapter 4: Lunch)*
9. **SHRIMP SALAD ROLL** *(Echo Lake, Disney's Hollywood Studios, Chapter 4: Lunch)*
10. **SPOON BREAD** *(Hollywood Boulevard, Disney's Hollywood Studios, Chapter 5: Appetizers and Snacks)*
11. **PARMESAN CHIPS** *(Sunset Boulevard, Disney's Hollywood Studios, Chapter 5: Appetizers and Snacks)*
12. **FRIED HERB AND GARLIC CHEESE** *(Echo Lake, Disney's Hollywood Studios, Chapter 5: Appetizers and Snacks)*
13. **FELUCIAN KEFTA AND HUMMUS GARDEN SPREAD** *(Star Wars: Galaxy's Edge, Disney's Hollywood Studios, Chapter 6: Main Dishes)*
14. **PORK ON PORK BURGER** *(Commissary Lane, Disney's Hollywood Studios, Chapter 6: Main Dishes)*
15. **GRAPEFRUIT CAKE** *(Hollywood Boulevard, Disney's Hollywood Studios, Chapter 7: Desserts)*
16. **WOOKIEE COOKIES** *(Echo Lake, Disney's Hollywood Studios, Chapter 7: Desserts)*
17. **COLD BREW BLACK CAF** *(Star Wars: Galaxy's Edge, Disney's Hollywood Studios, Chapter 8: Drinks)*
18. **YUB NUB** *(Star Wars: Galaxy's Edge, Disney's Hollywood Studios, Chapter 8: Drinks)*
19. **ORBITING OREOS** *(Commissary Lane, Disney's Hollywood Studios, Chapter 8: Drinks)*
20. **MOWIE WOWIE** *(Echo Lake, Disney's Hollywood Studios, Chapter 8: Drinks)*

DISNEY'S ANIMAL KINGDOM

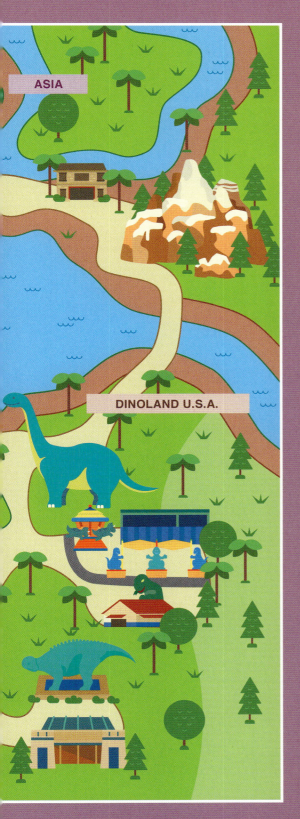

1. **MARSHALL'S FAVORITE SAUSAGE, EGG, AND CHEESE BISCUITS** (Pandora—The World of Avatar, Disney's Animal Kingdom, Chapter 3: Breakfast)
2. **LETTUCE CUPS** (Asia, Disney's Animal Kingdom, Chapter 4: Lunch)
3. **SMOKEHOUSE CHICKEN SALAD** (Discovery Island, Disney's Animal Kingdom, Chapter 4: Lunch)
4. **TIFFINS SIGNATURE BREAD SERVICE** (Discovery Island, Disney's Animal Kingdom, Chapter 5: Appetizers and Snacks)
5. **AHI TUNA NACHOS** (Asia, Disney's Animal Kingdom, Chapter 5: Appetizers and Snacks)
6. **ST. LOUIS RIB DINNERS** (Discovery Island, Disney's Animal Kingdom, Chapter 6: Main Dishes)
7. **SLOW-ROASTED SLICED GRILLED BEEF BOWLS** (Pandora—The World of Avatar, Disney's Animal Kingdom, Chapter 6: Main Dishes)
8. **HOT LINK BOWLS** (Africa, Disney's Animal Kingdom, Chapter 6: Main Dishes)
9. **FRIED WONTONS** (Asia, Disney's Animal Kingdom, Chapter 7: Desserts)
10. **CHOCOLATE CAKE** (Pandora—The World of Avatar, Disney's Animal Kingdom, Chapter 7: Desserts)
11. **HONEY BEE CUPCAKES** (DinoLand U.S.A., Disney's Animal Kingdom, Chapter 7: Desserts)
12. **FICHWA MAJI** (Africa, Disney's Animal Kingdom, Chapter 8: Drinks)
13. **RUM BLOSSOMS** (Pandora—The World of Avatar, Disney's Animal Kingdom, Chapter 8: Drinks)

DISNEY CALIFORNIA ADVENTURE

1. **AVOCADO TOAST** (Pacific Wharf, Disney California Adventure, Chapter 3: Breakfast)

2. **EVER-EXPANDING CINNA-PYM TOAST** (Avengers Campus, Disney California Adventure, Chapter 3: Breakfast)

3. **SLOW-ROASTED HAM, SWISS & EGG CROISSANTS** (Buena Vista Street, Disney California Adventure, Chapter 3: Breakfast)

4. **POBLANO MAC & CHEESE** (Paradise Gardens Park, Disney California Adventure, Chapter 4: Lunch)

5. **NOT SO LITTLE CHICKEN SANDWICH** (Avengers Campus, Disney California Adventure, Chapter 4: Lunch)

6. **CANDIED BACON** (Avengers Campus, Disney California Adventure, Chapter 5: Appetizers and Snacks)

7. **LOBSTER NACHOS** (Pixar Pier, Disney California Adventure, Chapter 5: Appetizers and Snacks)

8. **FRIJOLES CHARROS** (Pacific Wharf, Disney California Adventure, Chapter 5: Appetizers and Snacks)

9. **IMPOSSIBLE SPOONFUL** (Avengers Campus, Disney California Adventure, Chapter 6: Main Dishes)

10. **BEEF BULGOGI BURRITOS** (Pacific Wharf, Disney California Adventure, Chapter 6: Main Dishes)

11. **KA-CHEESEBURGER** (Cars Land, Disney California Adventure, Chapter 6: Main Dishes)

12. **STRAWBERRY SHORTCAKE FUNNEL CAKE FRIES** (Hollywood Land, Disney California Adventure, Chapter 7: Desserts)

13. **CELESTIAL-SIZED CANDY BAR: CHOCO-SMASH CANDY BAR** (Avengers Campus, Disney California Adventure, Chapter 7: Desserts)

14. **HAZELNUT CRUNCH MICKEY POPS** (Buena Vista Street, Disney California Adventure, Chapter 7: Desserts)

15. **PROTON PUNCH** (Avengers Campus, Disney California Adventure, Chapter 8: Drinks)

16. **PINGO DOCE** (Avengers Campus, Disney California Adventure, Chapter 8: Drinks)

17. **HONEY BUZZ** (Avengers Campus, Disney California Adventure, Chapter 8: Drinks)

18. **2319** (Pixar Pier, Disney California Adventure, Chapter 8: Drinks)

Standard US/Metric Measurement Conversions

VOLUME CONVERSIONS

US Volume Measure	Metric Equivalent
⅛ teaspoon	0.5 milliliter
¼ teaspoon	1 milliliter
½ teaspoon	2 milliliters
1 teaspoon	5 milliliters
½ tablespoon	7 milliliters
1 tablespoon (3 teaspoons)	15 milliliters
2 tablespoons (1 fluid ounce)	30 milliliters
¼ cup (4 tablespoons)	60 milliliters
⅓ cup	90 milliliters
½ cup (4 fluid ounces)	125 milliliters
⅔ cup	160 milliliters
¾ cup (6 fluid ounces)	180 milliliters
1 cup (16 tablespoons)	250 milliliters
1 pint (2 cups)	500 milliliters
1 quart (4 cups)	1 liter (about)

WEIGHT CONVERSIONS

US Weight Measure	Metric Equivalent
½ ounce	15 grams
1 ounce	30 grams
2 ounces	60 grams
3 ounces	85 grams
¼ pound (4 ounces)	115 grams
½ pound (8 ounces)	225 grams
¾ pound (12 ounces)	340 grams
1 pound (16 ounces)	454 grams

OVEN TEMPERATURE CONVERSIONS

Degrees Fahrenheit	Degrees Celsius
200 degrees F	95 degrees C
250 degrees F	120 degrees C
275 degrees F	135 degrees C
300 degrees F	150 degrees C
325 degrees F	160 degrees C
350 degrees F	180 degrees C
375 degrees F	190 degrees C
400 degrees F	205 degrees C
425 degrees F	220 degrees C
450 degrees F	230 degrees C

BAKING PAN SIZES

American	Metric
8 × 1½ inch round baking pan	20 × 4 cm cake tin
9 × 1½ inch round baking pan	23 × 3.5 cm cake tin
11 × 7 × 1½ inch baking pan	28 × 18 × 4 cm baking tin
13 × 9 × 2 inch baking pan	30 × 20 × 5 cm baking tin
2 quart rectangular baking dish	30 × 20 × 3 cm baking tin
15 × 10 × 2 inch baking pan	30 × 25 × 2 cm baking tin (Swiss roll tin)
9 inch pie plate	22 × 4 or 23 × 4 cm pie plate
7 or 8 inch springform pan	18 or 20 cm springform or loose bottom cake tin
9 × 5 × 3 inch loaf pan	23 × 13 × 7 cm or 2 lb narrow loaf or pâté tin
1½ quart casserole	1.5 liter casserole
2 quart casserole	2 liter casserole

Index

Air fryer, 26
Aluminum cream maker, 26
Appetizers and snacks, 93–121
    Ahi Tuna Nachos, 114–15
    Baby Iceberg Wedge Salad, 107
    Candied Bacon, 113
    Carpaccio di Manzo, 103
    Chicken Pot Stickers, 105
    Country Seasonal Salad, 100–101
    Five-Blossom Bread (pretzel knots), 97–98
    Fried Herb and Garlic Cheese, 110–12
    Fried Mozzarella, 106
    Fried Pickles, 94–95
    Frijoles Charros, 116
    House-Made Peach Applesauce, 102
    Lobster Nachos, 120–21
    Parmesan Chips, 109
    Pomme Frites, 99
    Spoon Bread, 108
    Tiffins Signature Bread Service, 117–19
Apples
    House-Made Peach Applesauce, 102
    Johnny Appleseed's Warm Apple Cakes, 164–65
Avocado Toast, 58–59
Award Wieners, 181–83

Backlot Express, 172–74
Bacon
    American Breakfast Burrito, 41
    Breakfast Sandwich, 44
    Candied Bacon, 113
    Savoyarde Galette, 137
Bacon press, 26
Baking sheets, 26

Bananas
    Banana Cream Topping, 177
    Peanut Butter, Chocolate-Hazelnut Spread, and Banana Sandwich, 75
    Sweet Lumpia!, 155
Beans
    Felucian Kefta and Hummus Garden Spread, 141–43
    Frijoles Charros, 116
    "Totchos," 82–83
Beef
    Beef Bulgogi Burritos, 147
    Breakfast Bowls, 54
    Carpaccio di Manzo, 103
    Cranberry Roasted Medallion of Angus Beef Filet, 135
    Ka-Cheeseburger, 150–51
    Slow-Roasted Sliced Grilled Beef Bowls, 140
    Tenderloin of Beef, 131
    "Totchos," 82–83
Bengal Barbecue
    Chieftain Chicken Skewers, 66
    Outback Vegetable Skewers, 67
Be Our Guest Restaurant
    about, 17–18
    Country Seasonal Salad, 100–101
    Herb-Salted Pork Tenderloin, 130
    House-Made Peach Applesauce, 102
Berries
    Berry Short Cake, 168
    Black Magic, 200–201
    Country Seasonal Salad, 100–101
    Happy Haunts Milk Shake, 197
    Meiloorun Juice, 193
    Raspberry Sauce, 110
    Red Berries Sauce, 53

Strawberry Shortcake Funnel Cake Fries, 181–83
The Sun Bonnet Trio Strawberry Salad, 72
Vegan Blackberry Cupcakes, 166–67
Blenders, 27, 30
Blue Bayou Restaurant, 194–95
Blue curaçao, in Fichwa Maji, 207
Bowls
    Breakfast Bowls, 54
    Hot Link Bowls, 146
    Slow-Roasted Sliced Grilled Beef Bowls, 140
Bread and pastries. See also Pizza and flatbread; Toast
    about: muffin pans, 32; pastry cutter for, 32
    Caramel Monkey Bread, 64
    Cinnamon Rolls, 46–47
    Cinnamon-Sugar Doughnuts, 50
    Classique Galettes, 51
    Croutons, 88
    Five-Blossom Bread (pretzel knots), 97–98
    Marshall's Favorite Sausage, Egg, and Cheese Biscuits, 56–57
    Mustafarian Lava Rolls, 42–43
    Spoon Bread, 108
    Tiffins Signature Bread Service, 117–19
    Warm Glazed Doughnut, 55
Breakfast, 39–64
    American Breakfast Burrito, 41
    Avocado Toast, 58–59
    Breakfast Bowls, 54
    Breakfast Sandwich, 44
    Caramel Monkey Bread, 64
    Cinnamon Rolls, 46–47
    Cinnamon-Sugar Doughnuts, 50
    Classique Galettes, 51
    Ever-Expanding Cinna-Pym Toast, 61
    Marshall's Favorite Sausage, Egg, and Cheese Biscuits, 56–57
    Melba Crêpes, 53
    Mickey-Shaped Pancakes, 49
    Mustafarian Lava Rolls, 42–43
    Sausage and Gravy Tots, 45
    Slow-Roasted Ham, Swiss & Egg Croissants, 62–63
    Warm Glazed Doughnut, 55
Bubble wrap, 27
Bundt pan, 27
Burritos, 41, 147
Butterscotch Pudding, 160

Cafe Orleans
    Battered & Fried Monte Cristo, 128–29
    Pomme Frites, 99
Cake pans, 27
Caramel
    Caramel Monkey Bread, 64
    Celestial-Sized Candy Bar: Choco-Smash CANDY Bar, 184–85
Caramelized Onions, 137, 138
Carnation Café
    Breakfast Sandwich, 44
    Fried Pickles, 94–95
Carthay Circle Restaurant, 187
Categories of dining. See Disney Parks restaurants
Cheese. See also Eggs; Nachos; Pasta; Sandwiches and wraps; "Totchos"
    Calabrian Cheese Sauce, 98
    Cream Cheese Icing, 47
    Fried Herb and Garlic Cheese, 110–12
    Fried Mozzarella, 106
    Ooey Gooey Toffee Cake, 159
    Parmesan Chips, 109
Chicken
    Chicken Pot Stickers, 105
    Chieftain Chicken Skewers, 66
    Jambalaya, 127
    Lettuce Cups, 86
    Not So Little Chicken Sandwich, 91–92
    Orange Chicken, 78–79
    Plaza Inn Specialty Chicken, 125

Smokehouse Chicken Salad, 88–89
Vegetable Korma (plant-based "Chick'n Strips"), 136
Chocolate. *See also* White chocolate
   Celestial-Sized Candy Bar: Choco-Smash CANDY Bar, 184–85
   Chocolate Cake, 176–77
   House-Made Chocolate-Chunk Cookie Sundaes, 156–57
   Mine Cart Brownies, 154
   Mustafarian Lava Rolls, 42–43
   Ooey Gooey Toffee Cake, 159
   Orbiting Oreos, 204
   Peanut Butter, Chocolate-Hazelnut Spread, and Banana Sandwich, 75
   Wookiee Cookies, 172–74
Cinderella's Royal Table
   The Sword in the Sweet (Sugar Cookie Sword), 161–63
   Tenderloin of Beef, 131
Cinnamon
   Caramel Monkey Bread, 64
   Cinnamon Rolls, 46–47
   Cinnamon-Sugar Doughnuts, 50
   Ever-Expanding Cinna-Pym Toast, 61
   Mustafarian Lava Rolls, 42–43
Citrus
   Coconut Lime Sauce, 117
   Grapefruit Cake, 169–71
   Lightyear Lemonade, 199
   Meiloorun Juice, 193
   Pingo Doce, 209
   Proton Punch, 210–11
   Rum Blossoms, 208
Club 33
   about, 22
   Cranberry Roasted Medallion of Angus Beef Filet, 135
Cocina Cucamonga Mexican Grill, 116
Cocktails. *See* Drinks
Cocktail shaker, 27

Coconut
   Adventureland Colada, 198
   Coconut Lime Sauce, 117
   2319, 214
Coffee
   about: coffee substitutes, 28
   Cold Brew Black Caf, 190–91
Columbia Harbour House, 197
Connections Eatery, 133–34
Cooking
   creating Disney restaurant experiences at home, 23
   equipment needed, 25–35
   getting started, using recipes, 35
Cooling rack, 28
Coral Reef Restaurant, 76–77
Cream maker, aluminum, 26
Crepe pan, electric, 28
Crepes/galettes, 51, 53, 137
The Crystal Palace, 160
Cucumbers
   Sweet Pickled Cucumbers, 69
   Tomato Cucumber Relish, 141

Desserts, 153–87. *See also* Chocolate
   about: Honey Buttercream Frosting, 179; ice cream machine for, 30; molds for, 31; pans for (*See* Pans); Vegan "Buttercream" Frosting, 166
   Berry Short Cake, 168
   Butterscotch Pudding, 160
   Celestial-Sized Candy Bar: Choco-Smash CANDY Bar, 184–85
   Chocolate Cake, 176–77
   Fried Wontons, 175
   Grapefruit Cake, 169–71
   Hazelnut Crunch Mickey Pops, 187
   Honey Bee Cupcakes, 179–80
   House-Made Chocolate-Chunk Cookie Sundaes, 156–57
   Johnny Appleseed's Warm Apple Cakes, 164–65

Mine Cart Brownies, 154
Ooey Gooey Toffee Cake, 159
Strawberry Shortcake Funnel Cake Fries, 181–83
Sweet Lumpia!, 155
The Sword in the Sweet (Sugar Cookie Sword), 161–63
Vegan Blackberry Cupcakes, 166–67
Wookiee Cookies, 172–74

The Diamond Horseshoe, 164

Disney California Adventure, map of restaurants by recipes, 227

Disney California Adventure, recipe-source restaurants. *See* Award Wieners; Carthay Circle Restaurant; Cocina Cucamonga Mexican Grill; Flo's V8 Cafe; Lamplight Lounge; Pacific Wharf Café; Paradise Garden Grill; Pym Test Kitchen

Disneyland, map of restaurants by recipes, 217

Disneyland, recipe-source restaurants. *See* Bengal Barbecue; Blue Bayou Restaurant; Cafe Orleans; Carnation Café; Docking Bay 7 Food and Cargo; French Market Restaurant; Galactic Grill; The Golden Horseshoe; Jolly Holiday Bakery Cafe; Oga's Cantina; Plaza Inn; Red Rose Taverne; Ronto Roasters; The Tropical Hideaway

Disney Parks restaurants. *See also specific Parks; specific restaurants*
    about: overview of, 13, 15; overview of author's perspective, 9; this book and, 10–11, 16
    categories of dining, 16
    closer look at specific restaurants, 17–22
    creating experiences at home, 23
    maps to find, 215–27
    Quick Service restaurants, 16
    Signature Table Service restaurants, 16
    Snack Carts (mobile/semi-mobile), 16
    Snack Stands (permanent), 16
    Table Service restaurants, 16

Disney's Animal Kingdom, map of restaurants by recipes, 225

Disney's Animal Kingdom, recipe-source restaurants. *See* Flame Tree Barbecue; Harambe Market; Pongu Pongu; Restaurantosaurus; Satu'li Canteen; Tiffins Restaurant; Yak & Yeti Restaurant

Disney's Hollywood Studios, map of restaurants by recipes, 223

Disney's Hollywood Studios, recipe-source restaurants. *See* Backlot Express; Docking Bay 7 Food and Cargo; Dockside Diner; Fairfax Fare; 50's Prime Time Café; Hollywood & Vine; The Hollywood Brown Derby; Mama Melrose's Ristorante Italiano; Oga's Cantina; Ronto Roasters; Sci-Fi Dine-In Theater Restaurant; The Trolley Car Café; Woody's Lunch Box

Docking Bay 7 Food and Cargo
    about, 21
    Cold Brew Black Caf, 190–91
    Tomato Cucumber Relish, 141

Dockside Diner, 84–85

Drinks, 189–214
    about: cocktail shaker use, 27; syrups for, 34
    Adventureland Colada, 198
    Black Magic, 200–201
    Cold Brew Black Caf, 190–91
    Fichwa Maji, 207
    Happy Haunts Milk Shake, 197
    Honey Buzz, 213
    Hurricane Cocktail, 194–95
    Lightyear Lemonade, 199
    Meiloorun Juice, 193
    Mowie Wowie, 205
    Orbiting Oreos, 204
    Pingo Doce, 209
    Proton Punch, 210–11
    Rum Blossoms, 208
    2319, 214

Violet Silk Martini, 202–3
Yub Nub, 192

Egg ring, 28
Eggs. *See also* Pancakes and crepes/galettes
    American Breakfast Burrito, 41
    Breakfast Bowls, 54
    Breakfast Sandwich, 44
    Ever-Expanding Cinna-Pym Toast, 61
    Marshall's Favorite Sausage, Egg, and Cheese Biscuits, 56–57
    Sausage and Gravy Tots, 45
    Slow-Roasted Ham, Swiss & Egg Croissants, 62–63
Electric crepe pan, 28
Electric pressure cooker, 29
EPCOT, map of restaurants by recipes, 221
EPCOT, recipe-source restaurants. *See* Coral Reef Restaurant; Garden Grill Restaurant; La Crêperie de Paris; La Hacienda de San Angel; Le Cellier Steakhouse; Lotus Blossom Café; Space 2020; Sunshine Seasons; Tokyo Dining; Tutto Italia Ristorante

Fairfax Fare, 109
50's Prime Time Café
    about, 20
    Fried Herb and Garlic Cheese, 110–12
    Mowie Wowie, 205
Flame Tree Barbecue
    Smokehouse Chicken Salad, 88–89
    St. Louis Rib Dinners, 144–45
Flo's V8 Cafe, 150–51
Food coloring, 29
Food processor, 29
French Market Restaurant, 127
The Friar's Nook
    Cinnamon-Sugar Doughnuts, 50
    Sausage and Gravy Tots, 45
Funnel Cake Fries (Strawberry Shortcake), 181–83

Galactic Grill, 41
Garden Grill Restaurant, 168
Gin, in Honey Buzz, 213
Glass (Mason) jars, 31
Glass pan, 29
The Golden Horseshoe, 156–57
Grapefruit Cake, 169–71
Grill or grill pan, 30

Ham
    Battered & Fried Monte Cristo, 128–29
    Classique Galettes, 51
    Savoyarde Galette, 137
    Slow-Roasted Ham, Swiss & Egg Croissants, 62–63
Harambe Market
    Fichwa Maji, 207
    Hot Link Bowls, 146
Hollywood & Vine, 64
The Hollywood Brown Derby
    Grapefruit Cake, 169–71
    Our Famous Cobb Salad, 73
Honey Bee Cupcakes, 179–80
Honey Buzz, 213

Ice cream
    Fried Wontons, 175
    Happy Haunts Milk Shake, 197
    Hazelnut Crunch Mickey Pops, 187
    House-Made Chocolate-Chunk Cookie Sundaes, 156–57
    Ooey Gooey Toffee Cake, 159
    Orbiting Oreos, 204
Ice cream machine, 30
Immersion blender, 30

Jackfruit, in Sweet Lumpia!, 155
Jars, Mason, 31
Jolly Holiday Bakery Cafe
    Cinnamon Rolls, 46–47
    Mine Cart Brownies, 154
Jungle Navigation Co., 198

La Crêperie de Paris
    Classique Galettes, 51
    Melba Crêpes, 53
    Savoyarde Galette, 137
La Hacienda de San Angel, 200–201
Lamplight Lounge
    Lobster Nachos, 120–21
    2319, 214
Le Cellier Steakhouse, 107
Lemon. *See* Citrus
Liberty Tree Tavern
    Declaration Salad, 71
    Ooey Gooey Toffee Cake, 159
Lotus Blossom Café
    Chicken Pot Stickers, 105
    Orange Chicken, 78–79
Lunch, 65–92
    Chieftain Chicken Skewers, 66
    Declaration Salad, 71
    Lettuce Cups, 86
    Lobster Bisque, 76–77
    Margherita Flatbreads, 81
    Not So Little Chicken Sandwich, 91–92
    Orange Chicken, 78–79
    Our Famous Cobb Salad, 73
    Outback Vegetable Skewers, 67
    Peanut Butter, Chocolate-Hazelnut Spread, and Banana Sandwich, 75
    Poblano Mac & Cheese, 87
    Ronto-Less Garden Wraps, 69–70
    Shrimp Salad Roll, 84–85
    Smokehouse Chicken Salad, 88–89
    The Sun Bonnet Trio Strawberry Salad, 72
    "Totchos," 82–83

Magic Kingdom, map of restaurants by recipes, 219
Magic Kingdom, recipe-source restaurants. *See* Be Our Guest Restaurant; Cinderella's Royal Table; Columbia Harbour House; The Crystal Palace; The Diamond Horseshoe; The Friar's Nook; Jungle Navigation Co.; Liberty Tree Tavern; Pecos Bill Tall Tale Inn and Cafe; Tony's Town Square Restaurant; Tortuga Tavern
Main dishes, 123–51
    about: plant-based meats and, 136 (*See also* Meat, plant-based)
    Battered & Fried Monte Cristo, 128–29
    Beef Bulgogi Burritos, 147
    Cranberry Roasted Medallion of Angus Beef Filet, 135
    Curry-Spiced Pizza, 133–34
    Felucian Kefta and Hummus Garden Spread, 141–43
    Herb-Salted Pork Tenderloin, 130
    Hot Link Bowls, 146
    Impossible Spoonful, 149
    Jambalaya, 127
    Ka-Cheeseburger, 150–51
    Plaza Inn Specialty Chicken, 125
    Pork on Pork Burger, 138
    Savoyarde Galette, 137
    Slow-Roasted Sliced Grilled Beef Bowls, 140
    St. Louis Rib Dinners, 144–45
    Tenderloin of Beef, 131
    Vegetable Korma, 136
Mama Melrose's Ristorante Italiano, 81
Maps, Disney Parks recipe locations, 215–27
    Disney California Adventure, 227
    Disneyland, 217
    Disney's Animal Kingdom, 225
    Disney's Hollywood Studios, 223
    EPCOT, 221
    Magic Kingdom, 219
Martini, 202–3
Mason jars, 31
Meat, plant-based
    Felucian Kefta and Hummus Garden Spread, 141–43
    Hot Link Bowls, 146

Impossible Spoonful, 149
Ronto-Less Garden Wraps, 69–70
Vegetable Korma, 136
Meiloorun Juice, 193
Mezcal, in Black Magic, 200–201
Mini loaf pan, 31
Mixer, stand, 34
Molds, 31
Muffin pans, 32

Nachos, 114–15, 120–21. *See also* "Totchos"
Nuts
Hazelnut Crunch Mickey Pops, 187
Peanut Butter, Chocolate-Hazelnut Spread, and Banana Sandwich, 75

Oats, in Wookiee Cookies, 172–74
Oga's Cantina, 42–43
Five-Blossom Bread (pretzel knots), 97–98
Yub Nub (drink), 192
Onions, caramelized, 137

Pacific Wharf Café, 58–59
Pancakes and crepes/galettes, 49, 51, 53, 137
Pans
baking sheets, 26
Bundt pan, 27
cake pans, 27
electric crepe pan, 28
glass pan, 29
grill or grill pan, 30
mini loaf pan, 31
muffin pans, 32
pots and, recommended, 33
wok, 35
Paradise Garden Grill, 87
Parchment paper, 32
Pasta
Impossible Spoonful, 149
Poblano Mac & Cheese, 87

Pastries. *See* Bread and pastries
Pastry cutter, 32
Peaches, in House-Made Peach Applesauce, 102
Pecos Bill Tall Tale Inn and Cafe, 72
Peppers
Outback Vegetable Skewers, 67
Poblano Mac & Cheese, 87
Pickled Fennel, 84–85
Pickles, fried, 94–95
Pineapple and pineapple juice
Adventureland Colada, 198
Fichwa Maji, 207
Fried Wontons, 175
Meiloorun Juice, 193
2319, 214
Pipette, 32
Piping bags, and tips for using, 32–33
Pizza and flatbread
Curry-Spiced Pizza, 133–34
Margherita Flatbreads, 81
Plaza Inn, 125
Pongu Pongu
Marshall's Favorite Sausage, Egg, and Cheese Biscuits, 56–57
Rum Blossoms, 208
Pork. *See also* Bacon; Ham
Herb-Salted Pork Tenderloin, 130
Pork on Pork Burger, 138
St. Louis Rib Dinners, 144–45
Potatoes
American Breakfast Burrito, 41
Breakfast Bowls, 54
Parmesan Chips, 109
Pomme Frites, 99
Sausage and Gravy Tots, 45
"Totchos," 82–83
Potato masher, 33
Pots and pans, 33. *See also* Pans
Pressure cooker, electric, 29
Pym Test Kitchen

Candied Bacon, 113
Celestial-Sized Candy Bar: Choco-Smash CANDY Bar, 184–85
Ever-Expanding Cinna-Pym Toast, 61
Honey Buzz, 213
Impossible Spoonful, 149
Not So Little Chicken Sandwich, 91–92
Pingo Doce, 209
Proton Punch, 210–11

Quick Service restaurants, about, 16

Ramekins, 33
Recipes, about, 35, 37. *See also specific main ingredients; specific meals/meal courses*
Red Rose Taverne, 49
Restaurantosaurus, 179–80
Rice
    Beef Bulgogi Burritos, 147
    Hot Link Bowls, 146
    Jambalaya, 127
    Vegetable Korma, 136
Rolling pin, 33
Ronto Roasters
    Meiloorun Juice, 193
    Ronto-Less Garden Wraps, 69–70
Rum
    Hurricane Cocktail, 194–95
    Mowie Wowie, 205
    Rum Blossoms, 208
    Yub Nub, 192

Salads
    Asian Slaw, 114
    Country Seasonal Salad, 100–101
    Declaration Salad, 71
    Lettuce Cups, 86
    Our Famous Cobb Salad, 73
    Shrimp Salad Roll, 84–85
    Smokehouse Chicken Salad, 88–89
    Spicy Kimchi Slaw, 69–70
    The Sun Bonnet Trio Strawberry Salad, 72
Sandwiches and wraps
    American Breakfast Burrito, 41
    Battered & Fried Monte Cristo, 128–29
    Beef Bulgogi Burritos, 147
    Breakfast Sandwich, 44
    Ka-Cheeseburger, 150–51
    Not So Little Chicken Sandwich, 91–92
    Peanut Butter, Chocolate-Hazelnut Spread, and Banana Sandwich, 75
    Pork on Pork Burger, 138
    Ronto-Less Garden Wraps, 69–70
    Slow-Roasted Ham, Swiss & Egg Croissants, 62–63
Satu'li Canteen
    about, 21
    Chocolate Cake, 176–77
    Slow-Roasted Sliced Grilled Beef Bowls, 140
Sauces, dressings, and spreads
    Buttermilk Ranch, 107
    Calabrian Cheese Sauce, 98
    Carolina Mustard Sauce, 138
    Coconut Lime Sauce, 117
    Creamy Strawberry Dressing, 72
    Honey-Mustard Cream Foam, 98
    Lavender-Honey Butter, 108
    Raspberry Sauce, 110
    Red Berries Sauce, 53
    Rémoulade Sauce, 84–85
    Seasonal Vinaigrette Dressing, 100
    Sweet Soy Glaze, 115
    Tomato Cucumber Relish, 141
    Wasabi Aioli, 114
Sausage
    American Breakfast Burrito, 41
    Hot Link Bowls (plant-based "sausage"), 146
    Jambalaya, 127
    Marshall's Favorite Sausage, Egg, and Cheese Biscuits, 56–57

Sausage and Gravy Tots, 45
Sci-Fi Dine-In Theater Restaurant
    Orbiting Oreos, 204
    Pork on Pork Burger, 138
    Warm Glazed Doughnut, 55
Seafood
    Ahi Tuna Nachos, 114–15
    Jambalaya, 127
    Lobster Bisque, 76–77
    Lobster Nachos, 120–21
    Shrimp Salad Roll, 84–85
Shaker, cocktail, 27
Sieve/sifter, 34
Signature Table Service restaurants, about, 16
Skewers, 34, 66, 67, 175
Snack Carts (mobile/semi-mobile), about, 16
Snack Stands (permanent), about, 16
Soup, Lobster Bisque, 76–77
Space 2020
    about, 18–19
    Lightyear Lemonade, 199
Squash, in Outback Vegetable Skewers, 67
Stand mixer, 34
Sunshine Seasons
    Vegan Blackberry Cupcakes, 166–67
    Vegetable Korma, 136
Syrups, 34

Table Service restaurants, about, 16
Thermometers, 35
Tiffins Restaurant, about, 19–20
Tiffins Signature Bread Service, 117–19
Toast, 58–59, 61
Toffee cake, ooey gooey, 159
Tokyo Dining, 202–3
Tomatoes
    Marinated Tomatoes, 107
    Tomato Cucumber Relish, 141
Tony's Town Square Restaurant, 106
Tortuga Tavern, 75

"Totchos," 82–83
The Trolley Car Café, 62–63
The Tropical Hideaway, 155
Turkey, in Battered & Fried Monte Cristo, 128–29
Tutto Italia Ristorante, 103

Vegetables
    Outback Vegetable Skewers, 67
    Vegetable Korma, 136
Vodka, in Violet Silk Martini, 202–3

White chocolate
    Celestial-Sized Candy Bar: Choco-Smash CANDY Bar, 184–85
    Honey Bee Cupcakes, 179–80
    other recipes with, 169–71, 187
Wok, 35
Wontons, fried, 175
Woody's Lunch Box
    Breakfast Bowls, 54
    "Totchos," 82–83

Yak & Yeti Restaurant, 86
    Ahi Tuna Nachos, 114–15
    Fried Wontons, 175

About the Author

As a child who grew up in Anaheim Hills, California, Ashley Craft could recite the Star Tours ride by heart and navigate the Park without a map,

Author photo by Valerie Salin

and she fell asleep to the sound of Disneyland fireworks each night in her bedroom. After two internships at Walt Disney World and many, many more visits to the Disney Parks, Ashley is now one of the leading experts of Disneyland and Walt Disney World. Her first book, *The Unofficial Disney Parks Cookbook*, was an instant bestseller. Today, Ashley lives in Minnesota with her husband, Danny; their three children, Elliot, Hazel, and Clifford; and their cats, Figaro, Strider, and Kelpie…but she still makes time to visit the Mouse. Follow her on *Instagram* at @UnofficialTasteTester.

THE MAGIC OF DISNEY— IN YOUR KITCHEN!

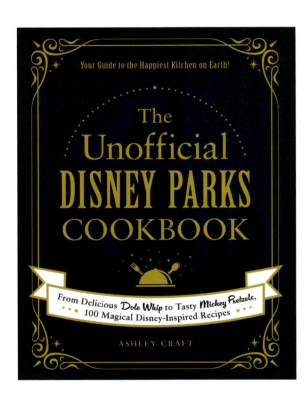 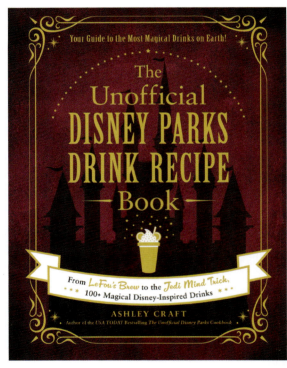

Pick Up or Download Your Copies Today!